50 FAMOUS CHRISTIANS

THE STORY OF 50 FAMOUS CHRISTIANS

© 2018 Colin Tinsley
ISBN 978-1-909751-82-8

The stories and pictures from all these missionaries have been compiled and collected from many different sources namely Wikipedia and various books and websites. If any copyright has been infringed upon, it has been without intention and we sincerely apologise.

Published by

www.hopeforyouthministries.org

Colin Tinsley
6 Hawthorn Hill, Kinallen, Dromore,
Co. Down, BT25 2HY, Northern Ireland
Email hopeforyouthministries@gmail.com
Web www.hopeforyouthministries.org

Contents

Amy Carmichael

16 December 1867 – 18 January 1951 (83 years)

Amy Carmichael was born in the small village of Millisle in Northern Ireland. In her late teens, she started a Bible Class for 'Shawlies' (mill girls who wore shawls) in a hall that belonged to the church she attended. Many girls attended her meetings and before long they had to buy a bigger hall that could seat 500.

In her mid-20's Amy felt called to overseas ministry and applied to the China Inland Mission. She trained at their headquarters in London but ended up going to Dohnavur in southern India with the Church (of England) Missionary Society instead.

When Amy arrived in India she was horrified to see young girls being forced to work as slaves in Hindu temples. Immediately she started to rescue them one at a time and soon she had to build an orphanage to house them.

In her writings, Amy tells how as a young girl she really desired blue eyes, rather than the brown ones she was born with. After hearing in Sunday school that God always answers prayer, she prayed for months that God would make her eyes blue – but that didn't happen! Years later she realised that God had purposely given her brown eyes so she could disguise herself as an Indian woman when rescuing the children – though she still had to dye her skin dark with coffee!

In 1931 Amy was severely injured after a fall and was bedridden for the majority of her final 20 years. She didn't let it discourage her but rather used the time to write 16 inspirational books.

When Amy died at the age of 83 she had served the Lord in India for 55 years without a single furlough. During that time she rescued over 1,000 girls from abuse and many of them later put their trust in Christ. Her example inspired many others to become missionaries including Jim and Elisabeth Elliot.

Amy Carmichael

```
L D K D E C N I V N O C P C Y
H P C V N F I M Z F K C F J U
M U A O R P H A N A G E W M K
K O Y U O T L U L Y P P X R B
A V G Y K A W B M K B V O A W
E F O U N D E D Y M X W S H Y
P N O I S S I M J C D J I M R
Z I F S U F F E R I N G H W A
C G D F N M P C W F D N N T N
A A B H W W Z W P V M C Y A O
A A R B W C A J S S E R D S I
I N A L L E A H C I M R A C S
D I M W N A R Q D I V T F Q S
N H Y A J K G N I L L A C C I
I C E G A U G N A L O R D K M
```

SUFFERING	DRESS	LANGUAGE	AMY	MISSION
CARMICHAEL	MISSIONARY	INDIA	ORPHANAGE	FOUNDED
CONVINCED	CALLING	LORD	WORK	CHINA

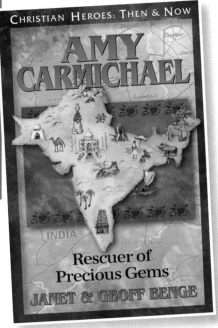

'Let nothing be said about anyone unless it passes rough the three sieves: is it true? Kind? Necessary?'

AMY CARMICHAEL: BEAUTY FOR ASHES BY IAIN H. MURRAY

Amy Carmichael

CHRISTIAN HEROES: THEN & NOW

AMY CARMICHAEL

INDIA

Rescuer of Precious Gems

JANET & GEOFF BENGE

5

Give me the Love that leads the way The Faith that nothing can dismay The Hope no disappointments tire The Passion that'll burn like fire Let me not sink to be a clod Make me Thy fuel, Flame of God.

Amy Carmichael

We have all of eternity to celebrate the victories, BUT ONLY A FEW SHORT HOURS BEFORE SUNSET to WIN THEM.

-AMY CARMICHAEL

LET US NOT
BE SURPRISED WHEN WE HAVE
TO FACE DIFFICULTIES.
WHEN THE WIND BLOWS HARD ON A TREE,
THE ROOTS STRETCH
AND GROW THE STRONGER,
LET IT BE SO WITH US.
LET US NOT BE WEAKLINGS,
YIELDING TO EVERY WIND THAT BLOWS,
BUT STRONG IN SPIRIT TO RESIST.
...
Amy Carmichael

"You can give without loving, but you cannot love without giving"
~Amy Carmichael

Adoniram Judson Junior

9 August 1788 – 12 April 1850 (61 years)

Adoniram Judson was a missionary who served in Burma (renamed Myanmar in 1989) for almost 40 years. He is remembered for being one of the first American overseas missionaries as well as being the first known missionary to Burma.

When Judson was in his teens, his best friend died suddenly and the incident led him to dedicate the rest of his life to God. Then in his final year at school, he decided to become a missionary.

His first destination was India, but neither the local nor British authorities wanted Americans evangelising Hindus in the area. Eventually, the group he was with was ordered out of India by the British East India Company and each of them went their own way to seek other mission fields.

Judson ventured to Burma and set about learning the language. He already knew Latin, Greek and Hebrew, but it took him over 3 years to become fluent in Burmese.

After 12 years of fervent labour, he only had 18 converts. Nevertheless, he was greatly encouraged as he had written a grammar book for the language and had started translating the Bible.

During the war between the United Kingdom and Burma, Judson was imprisoned for 17 months. Officers, led by an official executioner, burst into the Judson home. They threw him to the ground in front of his wife, before binding him with torture thongs and dragging him off to the infamous, vermin-ridden death prison of Ava.

After 20 months there, Judson was released and the treaty signed with the British at the end of the war enabled evangelism to be carried out in other parts of the country.

By the end of his lifetime, he had established a number of Baptist churches in the land and had translated the entire Bible into Burmese.

Adoniram Judson

"THE FUTURE IS AS BRIGHT
AS THE PROMISES OF GOD"
— Adoniram Judson

Across

5. A country
7. The people of Burma
8. An old language
9. People who live in jail
10. A small community
11. A large country full of Indians
13. Devotion to something
14. New Christians

Down

1. A very serious time
2. Language of the New Testament
3. God's Word
4. The sound from a foreign country
5. A church denomination
6. Someone who takes the gospel abroad
7. Without socks and shoes
12. Adoniram's surname

Our prayers run along one road and God's answers by another, and by and by they meet.
Adoniram Judson

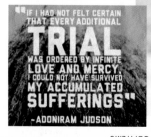

IF I HAD NOT FELT CERTAIN THAT EVERY ADDITIONAL **TRIAL** WAS ORDERED BY INFINITE **LOVE AND MERCY,** I COULD NOT HAVE SURVIVED MY ACCUMULATED **SUFFERINGS"**
-ADONIRAM JUDSON

MISSIONARIES

I will not leave Burma until the cross is planted here forever.

Adoniram Judson

Adoniram Judson's Last Words

"I am not tired of my work, neither am I tired of the world; yet when Christ calls me home, I shall go with the gladness of a boy bounding away from school."

CHRISTIAN HEROES: THEN & NOW

ADONIRAM JUDSON

Bound for Burma

JANET & GEOFF BENGE

THERE IS NO SUCCESS WITHOUT SACRIFICE.

If you succeed without sacrifice, it is because someone has suffered before you. If you sacrifice without success it is because someone will succeed after.

ADONIRAM JUDSON

The motto for every missionary, whether preacher, printer, or schoolmaster, ought to be 'Devoted for Life.'

Adoniram Judson

A.W. Tozer

21 April 1897 – 12 May 1963 (66 years)

Aiden Wilson Tozer was an American pastor, preacher, author and magazine editor. For his work, he received 2 honorary doctorate degrees.

Tozer was raised in a tiny farming community in La Jose, Pennsylvania. One day as a teenager, while walking home from his work at a tyre company, he overheard a street preacher say: "If you don't know how to be saved... just call on God, saying 'Lord, be merciful to me a sinner'." Upon returning home, he climbed into the attic and followed the preacher's advice.

As a consequence of the poverty he was born into, he was educated at home and taught himself what he missed out on at high school and college. Today, more than 60 books bear his name – the majority of which were compiled from his personal memoirs and sermons after his death. Many of his books impress upon the reader the possibility and necessity of a deeper relationship with God.

Prayer was of vital personal importance for Tozer. His preaching and writings were clearly extensions of his prayer life. He had the ability to make his listeners examine themselves intently in the light of what God was saying to them. In observing contemporary Christian living, he felt that the church was on a dangerous course toward compromising with 'worldly' concerns.

Tozer had 7 children: 6 boys and 1 girl. He chose a simple and non-materialistic lifestyle – for example, he never owned a car, preferring to travel by bus or train. Even after becoming a well-known Christian author, he signed away many of his royalties to those who were in need.

Over the years many people around the world have been greatly inspired and challenged by the life and sermons of A.W. Tozer.

A W Tozer

```
C F A J M J A K N P N D G L
H M P Y R S K O N C I W L D
K E A T N L H A A O T G A O
R N S I O J I U S M X N U Z
W T T N J T D K A M U I T C
J O O A S P K G V U E M I O
L R R I G R R N E N U R R N
H S R T V E O A D I O A I V
B H A S N A W C K T T F P E
C B U I Y C V I V Y O X S R
G I T R R H C R H R Z S O T
K B H H A E N E E W E V P E
O L O C M R A M K H R P N D
H E R H G L I A X C C E K X
```

TOZER	AMERICAN	CHRISTIAN	PASTOR	PREACHER
AUTHOR	SPIRITUAL	MENTOR	WORK	FARMING
COMMUNITY	CONVERTED	CHRISTIANITY	SAVED	BIBLE

"Spiritual Christians look upon the world not as a playground but as a battleground."
— A. W. Tozer

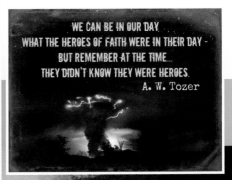

WE CAN BE IN OUR DAY, WHAT THE HEROES OF FAITH WERE IN THEIR DAY - BUT REMEMBER AT THE TIME... THEY DIDN'T KNOW THEY WERE HEROES.
A. W. Tozer

It is doubtful whether God can bless a man greatly until He has hurt him deeply.

Refuse to be average. Let your heart soar as high as it will.

A.W. Tozer

What comes into our minds when we think about God is the most important thing about us.

A. W. Tozer

"God is looking for people through whom He can do the impossible, what a pity that we plan only the things we can do by ourselves."

—A.W. Tozer

"We must never rest until everything inside us worships God."
A.W. Tozer

ACQUAINT THYSELF WITH GOD.

A.W. TOZER

I WANT THE PRESENCE OF GOD HIMSELF, OR I DON'T WANT ANYTHING AT ALL TO DO WITH RELIGION ... I WANT ALL THAT GOD HAS OR I DON'T WANT ANY."
- TOZER

"When I understand that everything happening to me is to make me more Christlike, it resolves a great deal of anxiety."
~A.W. Tozer

Billy Sunday

19 November 1862 – 6 November 1935 (72 years)

Billy Sunday was an American athlete and baseball player who became one of the most revered and influential American evangelists at the beginning of the 20th century.

Billy's father died when he was only 10 years old. He was sent to an orphanage where he was taught good habits, received a decent education and discovered he was a natural athlete. In the sporting scene, Billy's personality, demeanour and athleticism made him popular with fans, as well as with his teammates.

One Sunday afternoon when he was out for a walk he came to a street corner where a gospel open-air meeting was taking place. He was attracted by the hymns, which he had heard his mother sing many years earlier. The group invited Billy to their services and after counsel to deal with some inner-struggles, Billy committed his life to the Lord.

Following his conversion, Billy publicly denounced drinking, swearing and gambling. The change in his behaviour was noticed by both his teammates and fans. For 3 years, Billy visited the sick, prayed with the troubled, counselled the suicidal and visited public houses to invite people along to gospel meetings.

Billy also made use of his popularity and reputation as a baseball player to attract people along to his meetings. From 1910, Billy began to travel around different cities to conduct gospel missions. Often he would remain in one city for over a month, although on other occasions he preached at special one-off events to thousands of people.

Over the course of his career, Billy preached to millions of people – on most occasions without a microphone. After his death, it was estimated that Billy had preached nearly 20,000 sermons – that is an average of 42 per month!

God can use people who love sport to serve Him!

Billy Sunday

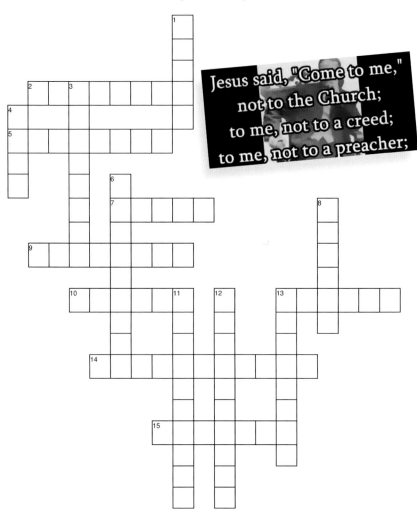

Jesus said, "Come to me," not to the Church; to me, not to a creed; to me, not to a preacher;

Across

2. An American sport

5. Nationality

7. Christian songs

9. Assemblies

10. A persons mum

13. Competitor

14. Persuasive

15. Competitor in running

Down

1. A boys name

3. Skirmish

4. Tread

6. Believer in Christ

8. Billy's Surname

11. A persons standing in society

12. Preacher

13. Proclaimed the gospel

Going to church doesn't make you a Christian any more than going to a garage makes you an automobile.

Billy Sunday

The reason you don't like the Bible, you old sinner, is because it knows all about you."

--Billy Sunday

ALL HELL CANNOT TEAR A BOY OR GIRL AWAY FROM A PRAYING MOTHER.

~ BILLY SUNDAY

C.H. Spurgeon

19 June 1834 – 31 January 1892 (57 years)

Charles Haddon Spurgeon remains highly influential amongst Christians of various denominations, who affectionately refer to him as the 'Prince of Preachers'.

Spurgeon was also a prolific author and wrote many hymns and poems, as well as publishing his sermons, an autobiography, Bible commentaries, books on prayer and devotionals, to list a few. Many sermons were transcribed as he spoke and were translated into other languages to be circulated around the world. Spurgeon delivered powerful sermons of penetrating thought and precise exposition. His oratory skills captivated his listeners at the Metropolitan Tabernacle in London where he preached.

His Christian journey began at the age of 15, when one Sunday morning on his way to an appointment, a snowstorm forced him to cut short his intended journey and he stopped at a little church. The text the preacher spoke on that morning from Isaiah 45:22, opened his heart to the message of salvation – *"Look unto me, and be ye saved, all the ends of the earth, for I am God, and there is none else."*

Later that year, he became a Sunday school teacher and preached his first sermon when he stood in for a friend. From the beginning of his ministry, his gift of preaching was obvious and his style was unique. At the age of 22, he got married and was the most popular English preacher of his day. However, that same year tragedy struck when he was preaching at the Surrey Gardens Music Hall for the first time. Someone in the large crowd yelled, "Fire!" The ensuing panic and stampede left several dead and Spurgeon was emotionally traumatised by the event. It had a sobering influence on his life and he often spoke of being moved to tears for no apparent reason.

Over the course of his life, he preached nearly 3,600 sermons and to this day, many Christians hold his writings in exceptionally high regard amongst devotional literature.

C H Spurgeon

```
Z C H R I S T I A N S P R A Y E R F F Y
M E T R O P O L I T A N C J Q U P D Y D
A M H J U C E X P O S I T I O N R E R P
B E C N I R P T G S Y J Z H K C O V O Q
M H Q K L L A I T N E U L F N I H O T C
A D S P U R G E O N A J N M U F T T A S
U S E I R A T N E M M O C D A I U I R S
S P E L L B O U N D M Q D U D L A O O U
T E A A Y D J J F Y G P D U B O U N G J
E P F Y Z N Q R E F R T T N A R L A H O
K U N M S S R E H C A E R P H P U L F V
E T R A E Q G G V G B S N O M R E S L K
```

SPURGEON	INFLUENTIAL	CHRISTIANS	PRINCE	PREACHERS
PROLIFIC	AUTHOR	SERMONS	COMMENTARIES	PRAYER
DEVOTIONALS	EXPOSITION	ORATORY	SPELLBOUND	METROPOLITAN

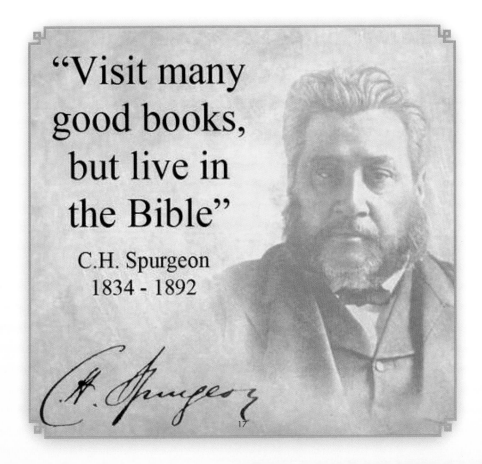

"Visit many good books, but live in the Bible"

C.H. Spurgeon
1834 - 1892

The Lord gets his best soldiers out of the highlands of affliction.

Charles Spurgeon

"Whenever God means to make a man great, He always breaks him in pieces first."

Charles Spurgeon

"Watch for God in the events of your life."

C. H. Spurgeon

"Do not rest until love and faith in Jesus are the master passions of your soul!" -C.H. Spurgeon

Charles Wesley

18 December 1707 – 29 March 1788 (81 years)

Charles Wesley was a leader of the Methodist movement in England and wrote over 6,000 Christian hymns. He was born prematurely and was the 18th of Samuel and Susanna Wesley's 19 children – although only 10 lived to maturity. In 1727, when he was a student at Oxford University, he formed a prayer group among his fellow students. They focused on studying the Bible and living a holy life. Other students mocked them and called them the 'Holy Club' and coined them 'Methodists' – because they were so methodical in their Bible study, opinions and disciplined lifestyle.

However, despite his zeal, it wasn't until the 21 May 1738 that Charles realised that good works alone could not earn salvation – but rather simple repentance and faith in the finished work of Christ. His brother John also accepted this truth and got saved 3 days later!

Following his conversion, Charles felt compelled to spread the gospel message to ordinary people and discovered his gift was writing poetic hymns that people could sing and remember. A year later, the two brothers took to field-preaching, after being inspired by the methods of George Whitefield – whose open-air preaching attracted thousands of people who didn't attend church.

In his hymns, Charles focuses on several doctrines: the personal indwelling of the Holy Spirit, the sanctifying work of the Holy Spirit, the depravity of mankind, and humanity's personal accountability to God. His hymns significantly influenced Methodism and modern theology as a whole.

Many of these hymns are still favourites amongst Christians today. Examples are:

And Can It Be That I Should Gain? *Jesus, Lover of My Soul*
Arise My Soul Arise *Jesus, the Name High Over All*
Christ the Lord is Risen Today *Love Divine, all Loves Excelling*
Come, Thou Long Expected Jesus *O for a Thousand Tongues to Sing*
Hark! The Herald Angels Sing *Soldiers of Christ, Arise*

Charles Wesley

```
S B K P V A N B C A N D H U K M
F H C X T Y B O H F P E W X E H
X F H K N G E L A D C O S T H T
D H G E E O K E R Z R E H S O W
E T M S M L I P L K T O I F E H
W G A K E O K S E N D L L S O C
E N N H V E G O S I G U L Q Z I
N E K U O H A G S N H E K S I O
E R I K M T R T E J Y I R W S W
R T N E E N O I S R E V N O C G
W S D M R P C H Q V L E A D E R
K T I R I P S C Z Q O Y L O H T
```

CHARLES	WESLEY	ENGLISH	LEADER	METHODIST
MOVEMENT	CONVERSION	RENEWED	STRENGTH	GOSPEL
MANKIND	HOLY	SPIRIT	THEOLOGY	WORK

Catch on fire with enthusiasm and people will come for miles to watch you burn.

Charles Wesley

I will SING a SONG NEW

Faith, mighty faith, the promise sees, And looks to God alone; Laughs at impossibilities, And cries it shall be done.

~ Charles Wesley

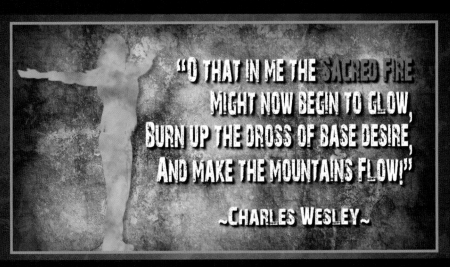

"O THAT IN ME THE SACRED FIRE MIGHT NOW BEGIN TO GLOW, BURN UP THE DROSS OF BASE DESIRE, AND MAKE THE MOUNTAINS FLOW!"

~CHARLES WESLEY~

Other refuge have I none;
Hangs my helpless soul on Thee;
Leave, ah, leave me not alone,
Still support and comfort me!
All my trust on Thee is stayed,
All my help from Thee I bring;
Cover my defenseless head
With the shadow of Thy wing.

(Charles Wesley)

Corrie Ten Boom

15 April 1892 – 15 April 1983 (91 years)

Cornelia "Corrie" Ten Boom was a Dutch watchmaker and Christian. During World War II, Corrie and her family helped many Jews escape the Nazi Holocaust before they were imprisoned for their actions. Her most famous book, *The Hiding Place* describes the ordeal in detail.

In May 1940 when the Nazis invaded Holland, a club which Corrie ran for young girls was banned. Subsequently, the Ten Booms opened their home to refugees – both Jews and other members of the resistance movement – who were being sought by the Nazi Secret Police and its Dutch counterpart.

On 28 February 1944, a Dutch informant named Jan Vogel told the Nazis about the Ten Booms' work. At around 12:30 that afternoon the Nazis arrested the entire Ten Boom family and sent them to Scheveningen Prison. Corrie and her sister Betsie were later sent to Ravensbrück Concentration Camp, a women's labour camp in Germany. After hard days at work, they held worship services in the camp using a Bible they had managed to sneak in. Whilst in Ravensbruch Betsie and Corrie were flea-ridden, yet Betsie praised God because for that reason the Germans didn't want to come near them! That left them free to have Bible studies in their barracks.

Betsie's health deteriorated and she died on 16 December 1944 at the age of 59. Before dying, she told Corrie, "There is no pit so deep that He [God] is not deeper still." A fortnight later Corrie was released and just a week later all the other women in her age group were sent to the gas chambers and died. Some time later Corrie was informed that her release was only because of a clerical error!

Corrie Ten Boom

```
Q W T F B B B S C L O H B G Y
I Y X D H I C N Q Z T U Q E M
K H L H U L B G K Z V E C R O
W G S I O A S L E Z H H N M M
Z U A G M L T K E S A F J A H
H E G V H A O H Q M C J J N Y
F I L H B E F C B U Y A H Y U
C L D V V N A E A Y M C P G A
P D L I K P R L Q U T C Y E S
D R W U N S P Z T U S S X T V
X P S A A G B B D H V T W O Z
V U N E T H E R L A N D S E Z
T Y C H G Q C F E I R R O C J
J Y Z R M T K N K J Q M O O B
D M W Y B R C Z O D M H S B K
```

CORRIE	TEN	BOOM	DUTCH	BIBLE
JEWS	HOLOCAUST	HIDING	GERMANY	GAS
CHAMBERS	NETHERLANDS	ESCAPE	FAMILY	HEALTH

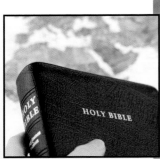

FAITH is like radar that sees through the fog.

~Corrie Ten Boom

"Worry does not **empty** tomorrow of its **sorrow.** It empties today of its **strength.**"

Corrie ten Boom

23

"Never be afraid to trust an unknown future to a known God."

~Corrie ten Boom~

When a train goes through a tunnel and it gets dark, you don't throw away the ticket and jump off. You sit stil and trust the engineer.

Corrie Ten Boom
Dutch Celebrity

If you look at the world, you'll be distressed.
If you look within, you'll be depressed.
But if you look at CHRIST, you'll be at rest.

Corrie ten Boom

"Let God's promises shine on your problems."

– Corrie Ten Boom

C.T. Studd

2 December 1860 – 16 July 1931 (70 years)

Charles Thomas Studd was a great sportsman and gained fame in his late teens when he represented Cambridge University in cricket. At the age of 19, he was promoted to captain his team and later represented England. He played in the famous series against Australia in 1882, which was the origin of 'The Ashes'.

Before attending University, in 1877 Studd became a Christian along with his three brothers at a Moody-Sankey open-air meeting. He said, "Right then and there, joy and peace came into my soul. I knew what it was to be 'born-again' and the Bible, which had been so dry to me before, became everything."

He encouraged Christians to be bold when planning missionary ventures and to completely trust in God to provide their needs. His spirituality was intense and he rarely read any books except for the Bible. Studd gave away his vast inheritance and pursued a career doing missionary work in China. He was one of the 'Cambridge Seven' who offered themselves to Hudson Taylor for service with the China Inland Mission.

Speaking of his missionary work, Studd once said, "Some want to live within the sound of church or chapel bell; I want to run a rescue shop within a yard of hell!"

After 9 years in China he returned to England because of failing health, but after recovering he travelled throughout India for 6 years as an evangelist. When he returned to England he became concerned that large parts of Africa remained unreached with the gospel. This led him to form the Heart of Africa Mission (now WEC International) and he devoted the rest of his life to spreading the gospel message across that vast continent.

C T Studd

```
Y G C K W I K T R C R T E N B L M N
E N C O U R A G E D R A Q Q O A X A
S S C R S R Y J N I B I H B R Y M C
H E L L Z T I G I N J U C H N U I I
F T N E E N G L A N D U I K E X S R
V E N T U R E S G K O O R N E K S F
B I B L E H W I A C H I N A L T I A
Q H F O V M I S S I O N A R Y A O S
I U U O Y Q M O O S T U D D W W N O
S P I R I T U A L I T Y C B N S S D
```

CRICKET	ENGLAND	STUDD	BORN	AGAIN
MISSIONARY	VENTURES	CHINA	INLAND	MISSION
BIBLE	HELL	AFRICA	SPIRITUALITY	ENCOURAGED

"Christ wants not nibblers of the possible, but grabbers of the impossible."

C.T. Studd

"IF JESUS CHRIST BE GOD AND DIED FOR ME, THEN NO SACRIFICE CAN BE TOO GREAT FOR ME TO MAKE FOR HIM."

C.T. STUDD   MISSIONARY TO CHINA, INDIA & AFRICA

LET US NOT GLIDE THROUGH THIS WORLD AND THEN SLIP QUIETLY INTO HEAVEN, WITHOUT HAVING BLOWN THE TRUMPET LOUD AND LONG FOR OUR REDEEMER, JESUS CHRIST.

• • •

CT Studd

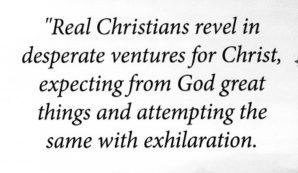

"Real Christians revel in desperate ventures for Christ, expecting from God great things and attempting the same with exhilaration.

C.T. Studd

"Had I cared for the comments of people, I should never have been a missionary."

- C.T. Studd

"ONLY ONE LIFE,
'TWILL SOON BE PAST,
ONLY WHAT'S DONE
FOR CHRIST WILL LAST."
CT STUDD
MISSIONARY TO CHINA, INDIA AND AFRICA

David Brainerd

20 April 1718 – 9 October 1747 (29 years)

David Brainerd was an American missionary to the Native American-Indians. His life became a source of inspiration and encouragement to many Christians, including missionaries such as William Carey and Jim Elliot.

He grew up with 9 siblings and became an orphan at the age of 14 when both his parents died within a few years of each other. He inherited a farm, but after becoming a Christian at the age of 21, he enrolled at Yale University to study for the ministry. At Yale, his health deteriorated when he contracted tuberculosis and he never finished his course.

Few modern missionary organisations would accept such a candidate, but on 1 April 1743 Brainerd started working as a missionary to Native Americans in Massachusetts. One day when the Indians drew close to Brainerd's tent they saw him praying on his knees. They witnessed a rattlesnake slither to his side and raise its head to strike, but then for no apparent reason, it regressed and slithered back into the brushwood.

Suffice to say, it's not surprising to read accounts of many other miraculous interventions of God on Brainerd's behalf and of mighty revivals he experienced among the idolatrous Indians in those short years.

On many occasions after he preached Indians came forward one after another, with tears in their eyes, to know 'what they must do to be saved...' It was an amazing manifestation of God's power working in them as His presence descended. Brainerd's centuries-spanning influence for revival is proof that God can use any vessel, no matter how frail, so long as it's sold out to the Saviour!

Brainerd laboured until late 1746 when worsening illness immobilised him and resulted in his death less than a year later, at the young age of 29.

David Brainerd

```
U R V I S L U O S P P E K O
T G J S N A I D N I T E D H
N Y R C M B U Q Y V H J W V
E D T G I B G Z Y C S F I N
M E R N O I T A R I P S N I
E H E I M T N E T C Y C E
G C V S N N L Q N X U O T B
A A N O L I D Q W C R U R S
R E O P G L A A E W P N U N
U R C T R O Z R D D S G O A
O P T O E F S I B W D J I K
C Q W M T A V P U I T X V E
N C M Y V A R C E E C N A N
E J R U D C J S G L X B S E
```

DAVID	BRAINERD	SNAKE	INSPIRATION	ENCOURAGEMENT
YOUNG	TENT	PREACHED	CONVERT	WORLD
SAVIOUR	TEARS	SOULS	INDIANS	GOSPEL

Here am I, send me; send me to the ends of the earth; send me to the rough, the savage lost of the wilderness; send me from all that is called comfort on earth; send me even to death itself, if it be but in your service, and to promote your kingdom

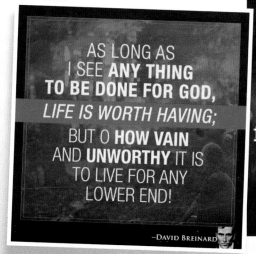

AS LONG AS I SEE **ANY THING TO BE DONE FOR GOD,** LIFE IS WORTH HAVING; BUT O **HOW VAIN** AND **UNWORTHY** IT IS TO LIVE FOR ANY LOWER END!

–DAVID BREINARD

If you hope for happiness in the world, hope for it from God, and not from the world.

– David Brainerd

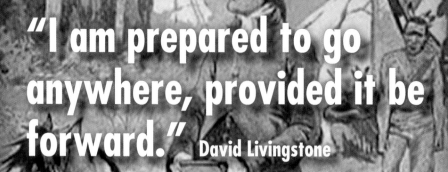

"I am prepared to go anywhere, provided it be forward." **David Livingstone**

Once more, Never think that you can live to God by your own power or strength; but always look to and rely on him for assistance, yea, for all strength and grace.

(David Brainerd)

LORD, USE ME AS THOU WILT; do as thou wilt with me: but oh, PROMOTE THINE OWN CAUSE!

David Brainerd

David Livingstone

19 March 1813 – 1 May 1873 (60 years)

David Livingstone was a Scottish pioneer and medical missionary in Africa and remains a national hero in Britain. Livingstone explored the African interior to the north and mapped almost the entire course of the Zambezi River. He was also the first European to see Victoria Falls at the border between Zambia and Zimbabwe.

As Livingstone travelled, he preached the gospel message but did not force it on unwilling ears. Although he is known as 'Africa's greatest missionary' he is recorded as having only seen one African converted: Sechele, the chief of the Kwena people of Botswana. Sechele was captivated by Livingstone and the message he taught. Being a quick learner, Sechele learned the alphabet in just 2 days and soon mastered English as a second language. When teaching his wife English, he translated the Bible into his native language. When Livingstone left the Kwena tribe, Sechele remained faithful and sent missionaries into surrounding tribes. After a few years he witnessed nearly the entire Kwena people getting converted to Christianity.

David Livingstone died at the age of 60 in Zambia as a result of malaria. His loyal attendants removed his heart and buried it under a tree near the spot where he died. The rest of his remains were carried, together with his journal, over 1,000 miles to England for burial at Westminster Abbey. While Livingstone had a great impact on Africa for the sake of the gospel, he did so at a tremendous cost to his family. In his absences, his children grew up missing their father and his wife Mary had poor health. His one regret in later life was that he didn't spend enough time with his children.

David Livingstone

```
L F T Q D K M M Y W I S D J I
D O P Z O N I G J T A N B R K
E G I A H U S S L K I M D N D
T N O F V S S U Y Z R E E A E
R I N C D X I C E L A D R C H
E H E C W C O T A I L I O I C
V C E P M Z N L T N A C L R A
N A R Z M T A M D O M A P F E
O E U A C I R F A I C L X A R
C T X Q K Y Y Q G R V S E V P
L I V I N G S T O N E A M S T
F S E G A S S E M C P A D Y U
X F J Y H S E C H E L E C O O
N B E W F K V O S N E W F X C
L W C L T F N V M G J A M Q I
```

DAVID	LIVINGSTONE	SCOTTISH	PIONEER	MEDICAL
MISSIONARY	AFRICA	EXPLORED	AFRICAN	PREACHED
MESSAGES	CONVERTED	SECHELE	TEACHING	MALARIA

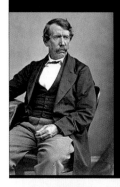

If you have men who will only come if they know there is a good road, I don't want them. I want men who will come if there is no road at all.

(David Livingstone)

"I will place no value on anything I have or may possess except in relation to the kingdom of Christ."

David Livingstone

There is one safe and happy place, and that is in the will of God.

David Livingstone

GOD HAD AN ONLY SON AND HE WAS A MISSIONARY.

David Livingstone, 1813-1873, missionary to Africa

"SYMPATHY IS NO SUBSTITUTE FOR ACTION."
-DAVID LIVINGSTONE-

I determined never to stop until I had come to the end and achieved my purpose.
David Livingstone

D.L. Moody

5 February 1837 – 22 December 1899 (62 years)

Dwight Lyman Moody was only 4 years old when his father, a farmer and stonemason, died at the age of 41, leaving his mother to bring up their 9 children on her own.

When Moody turned 17, he moved to Boston to work in his uncle's shoe store. His uncle encouraged him to attend church and it was there, at the age of 18, he became a Christian after his Sunday school teacher told him how much God loved him.

After a short time, he moved to Chicago and started his own Sunday school. A visitor observed him struggling to teach the class and commented: "If the Lord can ever use such an instrument as *that* for His honour and glory, it will astonish me!" Moody confessed: "I have got only one talent. I have no education, but I love the Lord Jesus Christ and I want to do something for Him." As a result of his tireless labour, within a year there were over 650 children attending each Sunday!

In October 1871, the Great Chicago Fire took the lives of 300 people as well as destroying Moody's church and home. The tragedy convicted Moody to press people to make a decision about Christ on the spot in case they didn't get another chance.

Thousands attended his meetings and when the managers of the Chicago World Exhibition Fair decided to open on Sundays, many Christian leaders called for a boycott. Moody thought otherwise and said, "Let us open so many preaching places and present the gospel so attractively that people will want to come and hear it." On one day, over 130,000 people attended evangelistic meetings coordinated by Moody!

D L Moody

Across

4. Labour
5. Moody's first name
6. First day of the week
7. Instructor
11. A gospel preacher
13. Teaching of the Bible
14. place where children learn
15. To remember something
17. An American city

Down

1. Dwight's Surname
2. Youngsters of parents
3. Born again
8. Transformation or change
9. Zealous in gospel preaching
10. A Christian organisation
12. Keeps on going
13. A city in USA
16. Creator of the world

"If I could relive my life, I would devote my entire ministry to reaching children for God!"

DWIGHT L. MOODY
EVANGELIST

Do all the good you can, to all the people you can, in all the ways you can, as long as you can.

– D.L. Moody

Some men's prayers need to be cut short at both ends and set on fire in the middle.

D.L. Moody

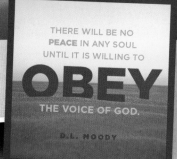

THERE WILL BE NO **PEACE** IN ANY SOUL UNTIL IT IS WILLING TO

OBEY

THE VOICE OF GOD.

D.L. MOODY

"The Bible will keep you from sin, or sin will keep you from the Bible."
-*Dwight L. Moody*

Out of 100 men, one will read the Bible, the other 99 will read the Christian.

D.L. Moody

Eric Liddell

16 January 1902 – 21 February 1945 (43 years)

Eric Liddell was born into a Scottish missionary family who served as missionaries in China. When he was the age to attend school, Eric was sent to a boarding school in England. He soon became known as 'The Flying Scotsman' as he was an outstanding athlete and won a trophy for being the best athlete of his year. At the age of 15, he was playing for the first XI cricket team and the first XV rugby team – and was subsequently appointed the captain of both. In his late teens, he attended Oxford University and was recognised as the fastest runner from Scotland.

He would later play international rugby for Scotland but running was Eric's passion. However, he is renowned for putting his religious convictions above the opportunity to compete in the 100-metre qualifying heats at the 1924 Summer Olympics in Paris. The reason Eric refused to run his preferred race was because it was scheduled for a Sunday. Instead, he competed in the 400-metre race, held on a weekday, and won.

Then, at the age of 23 he decided to become a missionary and returned to China to work at a rural mission station serving the poor. By 1941, life in China became very dangerous and the mission station was severely short of help. The missionaries were exhausted by the constant stream of locals seeking food and medical treatment. Liddell, who was then the leader of the camp, suffered many hardships himself, as food, medicine and other supplies became scarce. He kept himself busy by helping the elderly, teaching Bible classes and arranging games for the children.

Aside from two furloughs in Scotland, he remained in China until his death at a Japanese civilian internment camp in 1945.

It was said of Eric's unique running style at the Olympics: "People may shout their heads off about his appalling style. Well, let them – He gets there!"

Eric Liddell

```
N A D C D X H I A W S W Z X Z G B J D M
U J Z E Z F W E O A Q L S U N D A Y U M
L C R I C K E T R L V B M Z P E T H E I
R V P L C J N Q S I Y G E A R O X T R S
E M U I S Y J L G D C M A H Z E E Y O S
H Z F D S C O T L A N D P Z R L N H O I
C M N D E N I C I D E M V I H U Y N P O
A V I E I J A D U D Q Z M T C S G E U N
E L B L C H I N A Y Z S A Z E S A B P R
T J F L M I S S I O N A R Y S U T J Y N
```

ERIC	LIDDELL	RUNNER	CRICKET	RUGBY
OLYMPICS	SUNDAY	CHINA	SCOTLAND	ATHLETE
MISSIONARY	TEACHER	MISSION	MEDICINE	POOR

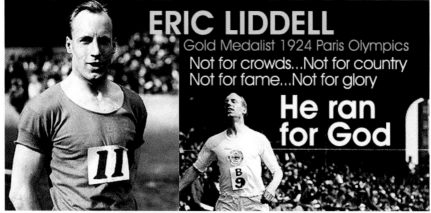

ERIC LIDDELL
Gold Medalist 1924 Paris Olympics
Not for crowds...Not for country
Not for fame...Not for glory
He ran for God

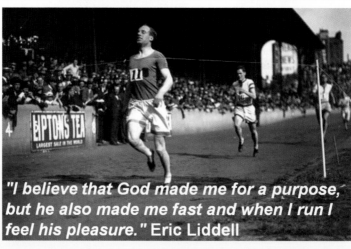

"I believe that God made me for a purpose, but he also made me fast and when I run I feel his pleasure." Eric Liddell

"CHRIST FOR THE WORLD, FOR THE WORLD NEEDS CHRIST!"

ERIC LIDDELL

If you are not guided by God, you will be guided by something or someone else.

Eric Liddell

Circumstances may appear to wreck our lives and God's plans, but God is not helpless among the ruins. God's love is still working. He comes in and takes the calamity and uses it victoriously, working out His wonderful plan of love.

— *Eric Liddell* —

Fanny Crosby

24 March 1820 – 12 February 1915 (94 years)

Fanny (Frances Jane) Crosby was one of the most prolific hymn-writers in history. Despite being blind, she wrote over 8,000 hymns and gospel songs, as well as being involved in teaching and mission work. At only 6 weeks old, she caught a cold and developed inflammation in her eyes that caused her to go blind. Then, at only 6 months old her father died, leaving her mother and grandmother to raise her. These two women grounded her in Christian principles and from the age of 10, Crosby memorised five chapters of the Bible each week. By the age of 15, she had memorised the 4 Gospels, the Pentateuch (first 5 books of Bible), Proverbs, Song of Solomon and many of the Psalms.

In her mid-teens, Crosby enrolled at the New York Institution for the Blind and was taught to play the piano, organ, harp and guitar. However, she realised her greatest gift was composing rhyme, which combined with her knowledge of scripture, enabled her to write deeply spiritual gospel hymns.

Crosby once described her hymn-writing process: "It may seem a little old-fashioned, always to begin one's work with prayer, but I never undertake a hymn without first asking the good Lord to be my inspiration." Her capacity for work was incredible and she was capable of composing up to 7 hymns a day! After writing a hymn, she would pray it would bring men and women to Christ.

In 1859 she gave birth to a little girl, Frances. Sadly Frances died in her sleep shortly after birth, which inspired Crosby to write the hymn *Safe in the Arms of Jesus*. Other well-known hymns she wrote include *Pass Me Not O Gentle Saviour*, *Blessed Assurance* and *To God be the Glory*.

She was quoted as saying: "If perfect earthly sight were offered me tomorrow I would not accept it. I might not have sung hymns to the praise of God if I had been distracted by the beautiful and interesting things about me. When I get to heaven, the first face that shall ever gladden my sight will be that of my Saviour".

Fanny Crosby

```
O E C N A R U S S A K F C W
E L V K T E T X Q D X J P R
E G F W U S U S E J G M R S
F I F C I D W J M Z K H U B
A E S R H S E Y E P P Y O L
S E H G O S P E L A N M I I
R C Q Z I X I P X W Y N V N
G E N T L E N S Z B Z S A D
J D L S O N G S S V C C S S
Y R V N Y E G O N G D I J S
I D H N Y N R W L X J I Z H
Z A C K G C N C O R E C S V
T I A G V P R A Y E R W X H
Y V U V K C K P F R P H W U
```

FANNY	CROSBY	HYMNS	SONGS	GOSPEL
SAVIOUR	BLIND	EYES	GENTLE	RESCUE
PRAYER	CHRIST	SAFE	JESUS	ASSURANCE

If I had a choice, I would still choose to remain blind...for when I die, the first face I will ever see will be the face of my blessed Saviour.

— Fanny Crosby

Blessed Assurance: The Fanny Crosby Story

1. Blessed as-surance, Jesus is mine! Oh, what a foretaste of
Perfect sub-mis-sion, perfect de - light, Visions of rap - ture
Perfect sub-mis-sion, all is at rest, I in my Saviour am

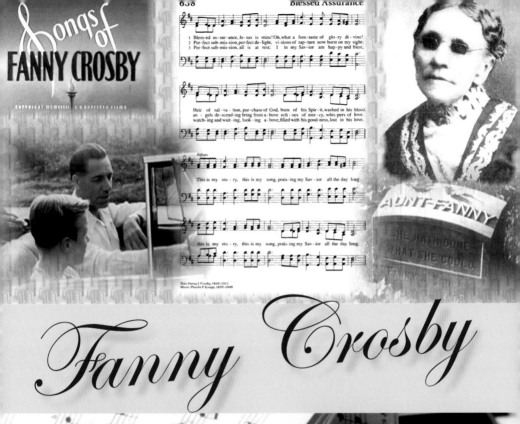

Fanny Crosby

Florence Young

10 October 1856 – 28 May 1940 (84 years)

Florence Young was a New Zealand-born missionary who established the Queensland Kanaka Mission (QKM) to reach labourers in Queensland, Australia with the gospel. She was the fifth child of an English farmer and was born in the town of Motueka, on the south island. In her early years she was educated at home, but was later sent to a boarding school in England to complete her education.

In her twenties, she moved to Australia and started working on a sugar plantation owned by her brother. There she organised prayer meetings for the families of the planters. Around 4,000 people attended them and they became known as the Young People's Scriptural Union. Increasingly she focused her attention on the Kanakas (Solomon Islanders), whose 'heathen' customs she detested. She began conducting classes in Pidgin English and used pictures to teach Bible stories, even using a butterfly's cocoon to illustrate the resurrection!

Her work spread to other plantations and was met with considerable approval from plantation owners and officials. In 1889, Government Inspector Caulfield noted that the behaviour of some South Sea Islanders had been improved by religious instruction. Florence stressed, "salvation before education or civilisation." She aimed to prepare the imported labourers for membership in their local established churches when they returned home.

In the 1890s, she spent 6 years with the China Inland Mission. Despite suffering a nervous breakdown, she recognised the work was preparation for the launch of the South Seas Evangelical Mission (SSEM). The mission was established in 1904 as a branch of the QKM. This was in response to pleas from Peter Ambuofa (an early convert to Christianity among the Solomon Islanders) and other repatriated converts who asked for support in establishing and teaching their own congregations. Young responded by leading groups of white missionaries to Malaita in the Solomon Islands to nurture the newly-established churches of her protégés.

Florence Young

```
A F Q S N O I T A T N A L P N
Y K G R C V R Q S B T W U A U
R Z N T N A U K N O M O L O S
A C I E G N O I S S I M D S J
N R H U X F I A L Y J W U A T
O S S V R L N L G H I A F L Q
I D I C L O L A D N P I R V Y
S N L H D R A J K L U H Z A H
S A B U Q E N R A L R O X T J
I L A R H N D N Q M U N Y I M
M S T C O C T C H U R C H O D
D I S H N E I L X L Z J P N S
Q Z E E R F R F T E A N I H C
Y T M S R F E W R Y X R T U U
X P Z Z F B Y W T P A U O V S
```

FLORENCE	YOUNG	CHINA	SOLOMON	ISLANDS
PLANTERS	MISSIONARY	SUGAR	PLANTATION	SALVATION
INLAND	MISSION	ESTABLISHING	CHURCHES	CHURCH

GOSPEL

BELIEVE CORNER CONSIDER ADDRESS

MINISTER MAJOR
WAY EVANGELISTIC TRAVELS
BELIEF SOMETIMES THEOLOGICAL TEACH VARIOUS INTERNET
BECOME
REFERENCE USED ACTIVELY AREAS
SPREADING CHURCH GEOGRAPHICAL FUNCTIONS CHRIST REGULAR TARGETS
PARTICULAR
SPECIFICALLY MEETINGS ROLES PREACHER ACTUALLY
EVANGELISM GROUPS ONE JESUS ENCOURA
BELIEFS STREET
USE
OFTEN KNOWN ENABLES BILLY PREAC
LIVING CALL
TICE SMALL EVANGELIST TITLE CHRISTIAN SAVI
SHARE SIMPLY REFERRED FAI
EN INCREASINGLY SET INFORMATION OTHERS
FOR TERM TELL EVANGELIZE PERSPECTIVES BASIS
PREADERS EVANGELIZATION WORD COMMUNICATION LISTENERS
TYPICALLY WORLD PREACHING COMMUNITIES PROSELYTIZE LARGE HOLD SCRIPTURES WHETHER
FOUND
TENTS
DONE GOOD CHURCHES CHRISTIANS PASS GOVERNANCE NEWS MANY PUBLIC REFERS CALLED
FIELD EVEN MISSIONARIES TOWN ONE-TO-ONE EVANGELISM CHRISTIANITY POSSIBLY HOME
MAY ASSOCIATED HUMANITY TRADITIONS SOMETIMES FUNCTION LEAD
NEARBY GRAHAM RELAYING BUILDINGS CULTURES ANYONE SPREAD
POSITION EXISTING FRIENDS
NEW ALSO SPREADS INTERNET

George Müller

27 September 1805 – 10 March 1898 (92 years)

George Müller cared for 10,024 orphans in his lifetime and provided an education to the children in his care. He also established 117 schools which offered Christian education to over 120,000 children, many of whom were also orphans.

Müller was born in Germany and was rebellious as a teenager but became a Christian when he was 20, after attending a Bible study. In 1829 he moved to England to commence missionary work and in 1836 he opened his first orphanage in Bristol.

Müller never made public requests for financial support, nor did he ever go into debt. Rather he had faith in God and trusted Him to meet his every need. Often food donations arrived just hours before they were needed to feed the children. On one occasion, with all the children sitting at the table, he gave thanks for breakfast even though there was no food! Just as he finished praying, a baker knocked on the door with sufficient fresh bread to feed everyone and a moment later the milkman's cart broke down outside the orphanage giving them plenty of fresh milk!

Every morning after breakfast, the children gathered for a time of Bible reading and prayer. When they reached the age to leave the orphanage, every child was given a Bible of their own to keep.

During his lifetime Müller travelled over 200,000 miles to many countries across the world, which was an incredible achievement before aeroplanes were invented! His language abilities allowed him to preach in English, French and German. Once while crossing the Atlantic, the ship he was travelling on ran into dense fog and had to slow down. Müller had an important engagement he didn't want to miss, so he took the ship's captain into a room and prayed the fog would lift. When they left the room 5 minutes later the fog was completely gone and the astonished captain became a Christian shortly afterwards!

Müller's faith in God grew stronger every day as he spent hours reading the Bible and praying. It was his practice to read the Bible completely through 4 times each year.

George Müller

```
G K B Q W E O R P H A N A G E D F I
I G W E D U C A T I O N S C H O O L
R R E C H R I S T I A N B F R R A J
L E G G W H E R J A L R S P A S Q T
S L R Q F Q X B J D E S H V F I A O
A L O W O D O O F A Y A L E B U T L
E U E W G D O W D O N A A U Y M F H
U M G Z K L I M B S C A P T A I N Q
```

GEORGE	MULLER	ORPHANS	ORPHANAGE	FOOD
BREAD	MILK	SCHOOL	EDUCATION	BOYS
GIRLS	FOG	CAPTAIN	CHRISTIAN	FAITH

GOD IS OUR BANKER & IN HIM WE TRUST.

THE ONLY WAY TO LEARN STRONG FAITH IS TO ENDURE GREAT TRIALS.

- George Muller

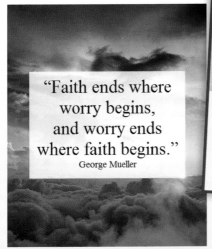

"Faith ends where worry begins, and worry ends where faith begins."

George Mueller

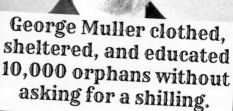

George Muller clothed, sheltered, and educated 10,000 orphans without asking for a shilling.

The greater the trial, the sweeter the victory.

George Müller

"Here is the great secret of success. Work with all your might; but trust not in the least in your work. Pray with all your might for the blessing of God; but work, at the same time, with all diligence, with all patience, with all perseverance. Pray then, and work. Work and pray. And still again pray, and then work. And so on all the days of your life. The result will surely be, abundant blessing. Whether you see much fruit or little fruit, such kind of service will be blessed..." - George Muller

I hope in God, I pray on, and look yet for the answer. They are not converted yet, but they will be.

— George Muller

"Only a life of prayer and meditation will render a vessel ready for the Master's use." - George Mueller

George Whitefield

27 December 1714 – 30 September 1770 (55 years)

George Whitefield grew up in Gloucester, England, as the youngest of 7 children. When he was just 2 years old his father died, leaving his mother to bring up the family on her own. At the age of 12, George left school and started working to help support his family, but continued studying alone in the evenings so he could attend University. He was accepted to Oxford and it was there he met Charles and John Wesley, forming a friendship that God would use on both sides of the Atlantic to influence multitudes with the gospel.

After graduating, he was ordained as a minister and began to preach with amazing success. He was able to hold an audience's attention with remarkable power. As he preached in Bristol, Bath and London, his popularity increased. Multitudes of 'common people' who didn't attend church were greatly challenged by his preaching.

Then in 1738, George set off with the Wesley brothers for the first of his trips to America. Their labours instigated what later became known as the 'Great Awakening' across America – when God's Spirit swept across the nation and drew thousands of people to Himself.

He travelled on horseback and preached nearly every day, for months at a time, to large crowds. At the end of his sermons, Whitefield freely offered the gospel and declared: "Come poor, lost, undone sinner, come just as you are to Christ". To Whitefield, the gospel message was so important he felt compelled to use all earthly means to get the word out. At times he was so emotional and passionate to see souls won he shed tears publicly.

It is reckoned that over the course of his ministry he preached at least 18,000 times and was heard by 10 million people.

George Whitefield

Across

2. Son of God
5. Bible teacher
7. Riding a horse
10. A boys name
11. A children's care home
12. A major development
13. George's surname
15. Not closed

Down

1. Guilty of sinning
3. We breathe it every day
4. Fervent
6. A preacher
8. Wonderful
9. To derive
14. A large animal

It is better to wear out than to rust out.

- George Whitefield

How sweet is rest after fatigue! How sweet will heaven be when our journey is ended.

—George Whitefield—

The reason why congregations have been so dead is because they have dead men preaching to them. How can dead men beget living children? - George Whitefield

George Whitefield

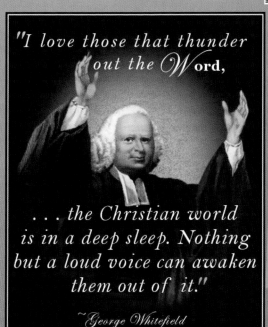

"I love those that thunder out the *Word*, . . . the Christian world is in a deep sleep. Nothing but a loud voice can awaken them out of it."

~George Whitefield

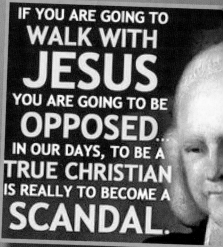

IF YOU ARE GOING TO **WALK WITH JESUS** YOU ARE GOING TO BE **OPPOSED**... IN OUR DAYS, TO BE A **TRUE CHRISTIAN** IS REALLY TO BECOME A **SCANDAL**.

Gladys Aylward

24 February 1902 – 3 January 1970 (67 years)

Gladys Aylward was born into a working-class family in London. She worked as a housemaid from an early age but always had an ambition to go overseas as a missionary. She studied with great determination and applied to the China Inland Mission. However, they reckoned at the age of 26, Gladys was too old to learn the language and complete other necessary training required for the mission field.

Despite being rejected she was undeterred and set out with her life-savings on a train journey to China. The perilous trip took her across Siberia where she was detained by the Russians, but managed to evade them with local help onboard a Japanese ship. She travelled across Japan with the help of the British Embassy, then boarded another ship to China.

On her arrival in Yangcheng, Aylward worked with an older missionary called Jeannie Lawson. Together they established a hostel called *The Inn of the Eight Happinesses* where they shared the gospel message with travellers.

Aylward became a Chinese citizen in 1936 and was a respected figure amongst the people. She took in orphans and adopted several herself. On one occasion she risked her life when she intervened in a dangerous prison riot and subsequently campaigned to improve prison conditions. In 1938, when the region was invaded by Japanese forces, Aylward led over 100 orphans to safety through the mountains, despite being wounded herself. She not only led them to safety but personally cared for them and led many of them to Christ. She never married, but spent her entire life devoted to Christ and winning others for Him in the land of China.

Gladys Aylward

```
A C I T Q A O H F M A N I H C L
I Y B J M K N W D F K S K Q U Y
K H D J E Y C P M E L G V L D Z
J O Q B K F J F G S D O W L M T
M W V N I V W S B Y A A W M C E
O B Q T S N K A R L U D V O H S
U M I W J E A A J X E H G N R D
N A L H U D N D S R J P U X I E
T M R H D O Y S E P S A S N S D
A B Q H I W T N D Q Z Y P O T N
I I X S A V J M J P U Q D A G U
N T S Q D R A W L Y A A L A N O
S I E S E N I H C L O E T W L W
M O U R X Y R C I B U T A E Q G
J N O I T A N I M R E T E D S W
P O J Y C I F S N A H P R O T A
```

GLADYS	AYLWARD	MISSIONARY	DETERMINATION	CHINA
INADEQUATE	CHINESE	INVADED	JAPAN	ORPHANS
GOSPEL	MOUNTAINS	AMBITION	CHRIST	WOUNDED

Gladys Aylward
MISSIONARY TO CHINA

The eagle that soars in the upper air does not worry itself how it is to cross rivers.

Gladys Aylward

> "These are my people,
> God has given them to me,
> and I will live or die with them
> for Him and His glory."
> - Gladys Aylward, 1902-1970, Missionary to China

Gladys Aylward

Gladys Aylward
The Small Woman
with a Great God

Gladys Aylward
THE LITTLE WOMAN

Oh God, here's my Bible, Here's my money. Here's me. Use me, God.

Gladys Aylward

Helen Roseveare

21 Sept 1925 – 7 Dec 2016 (91 years)

Helen Roseveare was an English Christian missionary, doctor and author. She worked with Worldwide Evangelisation Crusade (WEC) in the Congo, where she built a hospital and medical training centre in the early 1950s. A couple of years later she moved north, to an old leprosy camp in Nebobongo and built another hospital there.

After a furlough break at home in England, Helen returned to the Congo in 1960. However, civil war broke out in 1964 and she was taken prisoner by rebel forces. She was confined for 5 months and endured brutal beatings and an assault which ended in a 'trial', after which she was to be 'crucified'. Helen only survived because of the intervention of the villagers whom she had previously cared for. After her release, she claimed that it was a privilege to suffer for Christ. She returned to England for 2 years to recover but returned in 1966 to assist in the rebuilding of the nation after the war. She helped establish a new medical school and hospital, as the other hospitals she had built before the war had been destroyed.

In 1973, Helen returned from Africa and established an international speaking ministry and began writing Christian books. Her life of service was portrayed in the 1989 film, *Mama Luka Comes Home*. Helen told a touching story about the prayer of Ruth, a 10-year-old African girl, who prayed God would send a hot water bottle to sustain a premature baby after its mother died during childbirth. Ruth continued to pray: "...It'll do no good tomorrow God, the baby'll be dead; so, please send it this afternoon!" That afternoon a package arrived for Helen – it was posted 5 months earlier and sure enough, it contained a hot water bottle!

Helen →

The Congo

Helen Roseveare

```
Z F D G D W X W H I K G B E T
Q J C D O R N T D S H V X P R
L D W J C O Y E D Z S O U M K
X H C K T R S R I L G E G A B
Q P H D O O O L H N J D Y C C
L Y R L R S R B O H U A R G D
R F I A I E P C X E G S A U E
K N S C A V E G O L C U N L Y
U Y T I F E L W S E R R O J Q
Z I I D R A K M P N E C I J H
E Z A E I R A U T H O R S H L
O K N M C E J H Z Z J G S R E
P X U L A Z J B Y I B F I T B
U R E N O S I R P T S M M Z E
U D N D M I H O S P I T A L R
```

HELEN	ROSEVEARE	CHRISTIAN	MISSIONARY	AUTHOR
CONGO	CRUSADE	HOSPITAL	MEDICAL	LEPROSY
CAMP	PRISONER	DOCTOR	REBEL	AFRICA

There really is no cost, only the privilege of serving the King of Kings.

Helen Roseveare

There must be nothing in my daily conduct that, copied by another, could lead that one into unholiness.

mis·sion·ary {noun}

Someone who leaves their FAMILY for a short time , so that others may be with their families for ETERNITY.

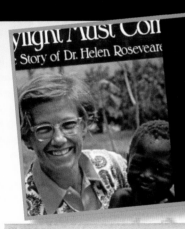

Story of Dr. Helen Roseveare

> God never uses a person greatly until He has wounded him deeply. The privilege He offers you is greater than the price you have to pay. The privilege is greater than the price.
>
> — *Helen Roseveare* —

If I truly believe in Him, I'll trust Him to desire for me that which is for my highest good, and to have planned for its fulfillment.

Helen Roseveare

We are called to reflect the Lord's beauty through our lives as much as through our words, and God will use this in His own perfect time.

Helen Roseveare

Hudson Taylor

21 May 1832 – 3 June 1905 (73 years)

Hudson Taylor was born to James and Amelia Taylor, a Christian couple who were fascinated with reaching people in China with the Good News of Christ. They prayed to the Lord for their new-born son: "Grant that he may work for You in China." At the age of 4, Hudson had caught the vision and apparently said, "When I am a man, I mean to be a missionary and go to China." However as a teenager, he ran away from the Christian beliefs of his parents, but after reading a gospel pamphlet entitled 'Poor Richard' at the age of 17, Hudson came to faith in Christ. Immediately, he started preparing for a future in China and spent his next few years studying the Bible and praying intensely, as well as learning the basics of medicine and the Mandarin language.

In September 1853, Hudson boarded a ship in Liverpool and set off towards China. He was headed for a country that was just coming onto the radar of the Christian West and only a few dozen missionaries were stationed there. He was able to preach in several variants of Chinese, including Mandarin, Chaozhou and the Wu dialects of Shanghai and Ningbo. The last of these he knew well enough to help translate the New Testament.

Taylor is regarded as being the most influential missionary to China and was the founder of the China Inland Mission (now OMF International), which was responsible for bringing over 800 missionaries to the country. They founded 125 schools which directly resulted in 18,000 Christian conversions. They also established over 300 mission stations with more than 500 local helpers in all 18 provinces.

In total, Taylor spent 51 years in China and is remembered for his sensitivity to Chinese culture and zeal for evangelism.

Hudson Taylor

```
M S N O I S R E V N O C E N M
T U S H A N G H A I M I G W D
T R D R D V A S T N E R A P M
D N A I F D V I N V V U U I U
B X D C N B U U T O V Z S F Y
G I C I T Z E B F S S S R Q D
K K T Q A S E M O O I D U G G
J A J Q X P T X A O Q R U B N
L L P E X R A S N N L T H H I
Z P I N V V Y D C E D O K C D
H E B R E W L E E E Z A X I A
X P H G S H O H L B N W R T E
P E T Y Q M R P X G B Z S I R
S K Q F H M F K D R A O B C N
Z A Z I C L E P S O G S R G H
```

HUDSON	TAYLOR	PARENTS	GOSPEL	TRACTS
MANDARIN	HEBREW	LATIN	SHANGHAI	ROBBED
MISSION	BOARD	CONVERSIONS	READING	CHRISTIAN

You must go forward on your knees.

— Hudson Taylor

" Would that God would make hell so real to us that we cannot rest; heaven so real that we must have men there, Christ so real that our supreme motive and aim shall be to make the Man of Sorrows the Man of Joy by the conversion to Him of many. "

Hudson Taylor

CHRISTIAN HEROES: THEN & NOW

HUDSON TAYLOR

Deep in the Heart of China

JANET & GEOFF BENGE

A LITTLE THING IS A LITTLE THING, BUT **FAITHFULNESS** IN THE LITTLE THINGS IS A GREAT THING.
HUDSON TAYLOR

God is not looking for people of great faith but for individuals ready to follow Him

"The devil can wall you round, but he cannot roof you in."
—Hudson Taylor

dream a dream SO BIG that UNLESS GOD INTERVENES IT WILL FAIL.
Hudson Taylor

THERE ARE THREE STAGES IN EVERY GREAT WORK OF GOD:
FIRST, IT IS
IMPOSSIBLE,
THEN IT IS
DIFFICULT,
THEN IT IS
DONE.

"God's work done in God's way will never lack God's supplies."
Hudson Taylor

Hugh Latimer
circa 1487 – 16 Oct 1555 (68 years)

Hugh Latimer was one of the three Oxford Martyrs who were burned at the stake under Queen Mary, as she sought to bring England back to Roman Catholicism.

Latimer was born in Leicestershire and was the son of a farmer, but after graduating from Cambridge University he became an influential preacher during King Edward VI's reign. He was an earnest student of the Bible and his sermons emphasised that men should serve the Lord with a true heart and inward affection, rather than just an outward show. Latimer's personal life also re-enforced his preaching. He was renowned for doing compassionate work, especially visiting criminals in prisons.

Under Mary's reign, he preached publicly on the need for a translation of the Bible in English. This was a dangerous move as the first translation of the New Testament by William Tyndale had recently been banned. Latimer was called before Cardinal Thomas Wolsey and given a severe reprimand.

Commissioners subsequently began to examine Latimer and other reformers such as Ridley and Cranmer. Latimer, hardly able to sustain a debate at his age, responded to the council in writing. He argued that the doctrines of the real presence of Christ in the mass were unbiblical. The commissioners tried to demonstrate that Latimer did not share the same faith as the most prominent bishops.

After a sentence had been pronounced, Latimer responded, "I thank God most heartily that He hath prolonged my life to this end, that I may, in this case, glorify God by that kind of death." A commissioner replied, "If you go to heaven in this faith, then I will never come hither, as I am thus persuaded."

Latimer was burned at the stake with Nicholas Ridley. He is quoted as having said to Ridley, "We shall this day light such a candle, by God's grace, in England, as I trust shall never be put out."

Hugh Latimer

```
P Z O L Y D N C B K A E G U H L U F R R
D U S P D Q S X Q W U I F X P A K R V C
A N O I T A L S N A R T P C A T W E F F
N O C C M G P Y E Z L S A O N I F M Q P
G I O B B P Y Q R E V N N I W M E R A Y
E T A I I U P W B O D C A K W E P O O O
R I Z G D B R E P L T L F A O R T F L F
O N E G X S L N E F P B R C J E Q E G G
U O Q K Z M U E E A I N Y K O M A R X H
S M R M A N L R H D I R W K A N A D F U
Z D J A Q T D C Z N N M E K D C G C Z G
I A K J H A S L G Y T I S R E V I N U H
```

HUGH	LATIMER	BURNED	STAKE	FIRE
REFORMER	DANGEROUS	TRANSLATION	BIBLE	CHAPLAIN
CANDLE	GRACE	UNIVERSITY	ADMONITION	WARNING

Play the man, Master Ridley; we shall this day light such a candle, by God's grace in England, as I trust shall never be put out.

Say the truth and shame the devil.

Hugh Latimer

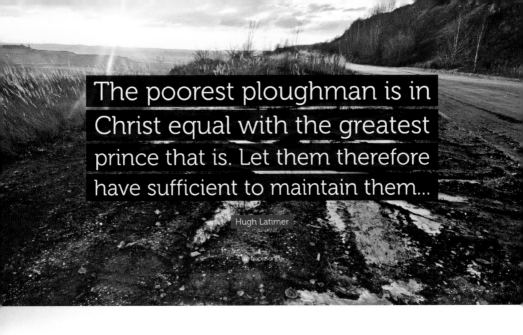

The poorest ploughman is in Christ equal with the greatest prince that is. Let them therefore have sufficient to maintain them...

Hugh Latimer

Say the truth and shame the devil.

Hugh Latimer

I.D. Sankey

28 August 1840 – 13 August 1908 (67 years)

Ira David Sankey was a renowned American gospel singer and composer. He often led the singing at big tent missions where the famous evangelist D.L. Moody was the preacher. Sankey used a lot of Fanny Crosby's hymns in their campaigns.

Sankey became a Christian when he was 16 years old at a revival meeting just 3 miles away from his home. When he was older he served in the US Army and fought in the Civil War between the north and the south.

In October 1871, Sankey and Moody were in the middle of a revival meeting when the Great Chicago Fire broke out. The two men barely escaped the burning city with their lives. Sankey ended up watching the city burn from a rowboat far out on Lake Michigan.

Sankey's first song was called *The Ninety and Nine*. Reading a newspaper one day, he came across a little poem that he liked and read it to Moody, but only received a polite reply. Sankey cut the poem out and put it carefully into his pocket. At a service later, Moody preached on 'The Good Shepherd' and asked Sankey if he had a final song. An inner voice spoke to Sankey and although there was no music to the poem, he placed the little piece of newspaper he had tucked in his pocket on the organ in front of him. Half-speaking and half-singing, he completed the first verse, which was followed by 4 more.

Moody walked over with tears in his eyes and said, "Where did you get that hymn?"

The Ninety and Nine became his most famous hymn from that time on.

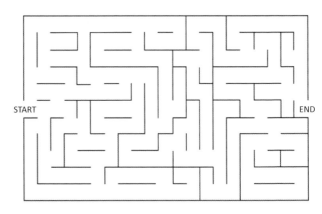

I Sankey

```
Z E P G A M E R I C A N K P E
N F R D O Y X P I Y R T T M W
O M E X O S O Y K Q E U S N S
R O A W B O P Q R A S N I N O
M W C F X W G E W M O E L O N
Y W H C S N A R L D P O E C G
A T E V Z V E C R Y M C G O S
F E D S B G U E X B O K N N O
E X K T N Y H W G I C H A V C
U P D I D P Y E K N A S V E H
N P S O E Y R L G U D C E R I
T B O H H J J Y D S L E I T C
G M S K L T W Q S N Z M Y E A
Q P R I U S S E N T V V M D G
W D E R W Q L A V I V E R B O
```

SANKEY	GOSPEL	SINGER	SONGS	COMPOSER
REVIVAL	MOODY	EVANGELIST	PREACHED	GOOD
SHEPHERD	TUNE	CONVERTED	AMERICAN	CHICAGO

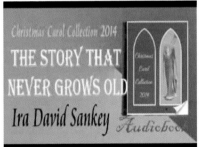

Christmas Carol Collection 2014
THE STORY THAT
NEVER GROWS OLD
Ira David Sankey

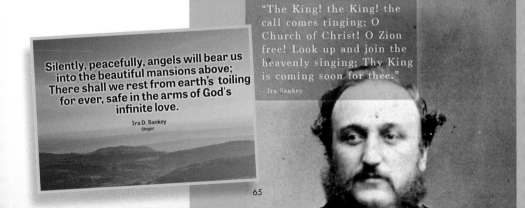

"The King! the King! the call comes ringing; O Church of Christ! O Zion free! Look up and join the heavenly singing; Thy King is coming soon for thee."
Ira Sankey

Silently, peacefully, angels will bear us into the beautiful mansions above; There shall we rest from earth's toiling for ever, safe in the arms of God's infinite love.
Ira D. Sankey
Singer

If you have singing that reaches the heart, it will fill the church every time.

IRA SANKEY

My Life
and the Story of
the Gospel Hymns

Ira D. Sankey

STANDING
STANDING

I'M STANDING

ON THE

PROMISES OF GOD

Isaac Watts

17 July 1674 – 25 November 1748 (74 years)

Isaac Watts was an English Christian minister, hymn-writer and theologian. He is recognised as the 'Father of English Hymnody' and is credited with some 750 hymns. Many of his hymns remain in use today and have been translated into numerous languages.

Watts was not the first Protestant to promote the singing of hymns; however, his abundant hymn-writing helped usher in a new era of English worship as many other poets followed in his path. He also introduced a new way of rendering the Psalms in verse for church services, proposing that they were adapted and sung as hymns.

When I Survey the Wondrous Cross and *Joy to the World* are among Watts' most famous hymns. Many of his hymns are filled with solid biblical doctrine.

From an early age, Watts displayed a passion for rhyme. Once when asked why he had his eyes open during prayers he responded:

*"A little mouse for want of stairs
ran up a rope to say its prayers."*

He received corporal punishment for this, to which he cried:

*"O father, father, pity take
And I will no more verses make!"*

Besides writing hymns, Watts was also a theologian and logician, writing books and essays on many biblical subjects. He also pastored a large independent church in London and spent a lot of his time training prospective preachers.

OH, SING
TO THE **LORD**
A
NEW **SONG!**
SING TO THE LORD,
ALL THE **EARTH.**
PSALM 96:1

Isaac Watts

```
V L A N G U A G E S J O Y D D
Z T C F C X H Y M N S N M R O
H E F N A F D K G U A G I W C
H T A X A I L S R I S S N O T
S H P D S X H V T W V D I N R
I E X V I L E S Q R H Y S D I
L O C R G Y I I J S P J T R N
G L R U N R Y D K A T T E O E
N O O W H E G T Z H Z T R U F
E G S C Y P A W A W V S A S M
P I S F D R R Q O O W M D W X
P A L E Z I C R P V H W A X R
U N O T T I L P R U K S K Z D
G J P E A D E Y D V Q L Y K L
I Y R Q G C C K G I T Z P I Y
```

ISAAC	WATTS	CHRISTIAN	MINISTER	HYMN
WRITER	THEOLOGIAN	LANGUAGES	JOY	WORLD
SURVEY	WONDROUS	CROSS	DOCTRINE	ENGLISH

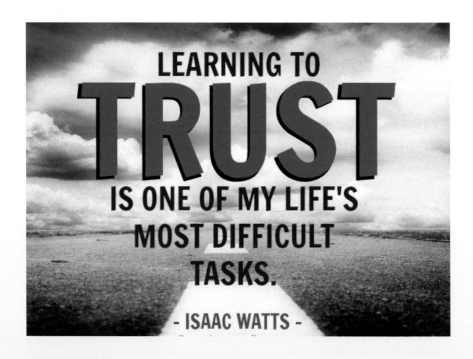

LEARNING TO **TRUST** IS ONE OF MY LIFE'S MOST DIFFICULT TASKS.

- ISAAC WATTS -

There's no repentance in the grave.

Isaac Watts

Were the whole realm of nature mine, That were a present far too small: Love so amazing, so divine Demands my soul, my life, my all.

"Joy to the world, the Lord is come!
Let earth receive her King;
let every heart prepare Him room..."
-Isaac Watts-

Birds in their little nest agree; and 'Tis a shameful sight, when children of one family fall out, and chide, and fight.

(Isaac Watts)

Jan Hus
circa 1369 – 6 July 1415 (46 years)

Jan Hus was born to peasant parents in the area which today is the Czech Republic. He is considered to be the first church reformer, as he lived before Luther, Calvin and Zwingli. His teachings had a strong influence on Western Europe and in particular on Martin Luther, who discovered his writings a century later.

To escape poverty, Hus trained for the priesthood. He said: "I had thought to become a priest quickly in order to secure a good livelihood and to be held in esteem by men." He graduated from college with a doctorate degree and was ordained as a priest in 1401 at Prague's Bethlehem Chapel.

He broke with tradition because his sermons were preached in the Czech language as opposed to Latin. Hus also spoke out against the sale of indulgences – a piece of paper that the church falsely claimed would ensure that a loved one who had died would go to Heaven. He also asserted that no pope or bishop had the right to take up the sword in the name of the church, but rather we should pray for our enemies and bless those who curse us. Finally, he added that man obtains forgiveness of sins only by true repentance – not by paying money.

Eventually, Hus was arrested and put on trial for speaking against the church. Hus protested and asked to be shown from scripture where he was wrong. He then fell to his knees and asked God to forgive all his enemies and was then burned at the stake for heresy against the doctrines of the church. His final words were "I am ready to die!"

His execution subsequently sparked a revolt and led to the Hussite Wars.

Jan Hus

```
S K B N U W L J F X L Z G V M N Y T
C C R S S E N E V I G R O F S D L J
Y Z M U Y M S S X G H Z W E D I A J
S R E F O R M E R A E C L U K N N W
E V H C T K E R B L D U R Z E A F S
R Z Q T H T G H Z V E E R U Q S T W
E S E C N E G L U D N I N T H T W S
H U K E C N A T N E P E R R A C H C
P S Y X L E C N E U L F N I U Q U Q
P R O T E S T A N T I S M P T B S Y
```

JAN	HUS	CHURCH	REFORMER	PROTESTANTISM
INFLUENCE	BURNED	STAKE	HERESY	CZECH
INDULGENCES	FORGIVENESS	TRUE	REPENTANCE	SINS

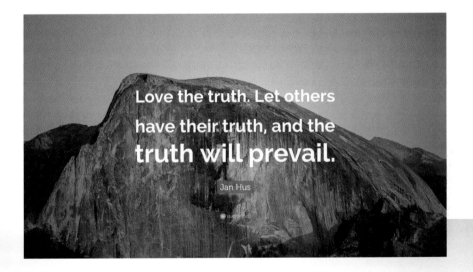

Love the truth. Let others have their truth, and the **truth will prevail.**

Jan Hus

What I have taught with my lips I now seal with my blood.

Jan Hus

Rejoice, that the immortal God is born, so that mortal man may live in eternity.

~ Jan Hus

For whoso dies for Christ, he is conqueror and is delivered from all misery and attains the eternal joy to which may it please our Saviour to bring us all.

Jan Hus

It is better to die well than to live badly.

-Jan Hus

John Hus
1369 - July 6, 1415

"Seek the truth
Listen to the truth
Teach the truth
Love the truth
Abide by the truth
And defend the truth
unto death."

Jim Elliot

8 October 1927 – 8 January 1956 (29 years)

Jim Elliot came to faith at the age of 6 and grew up in a home where obedience and honesty were expected. The Elliot parents encouraged their children to be adventurous and urged them to live for Christ.

In 1941, Elliot went to college to study architectural drawing. During his time there he joined the drama society, wrestling team and public speaking club. He used his speaking ability regularly and a classmate told how Elliot quoted the Bible to the Student Body President to explain why he would not be attending a particular party. Another time he risked being put out of the public speaking club for refusing to give a speech on politics because he believed that Christians should not get involved in such matters.

His parents and friends encouraged him to get involved in youth ministry at home in the United States, but Elliot felt called to international missions and in particular to reach the Auca (savage) Indians in Ecuador.

On 21 February 1952, Elliot arrived in Ecuador and started evangelising the Quechua Indians. In 1953 he married a fellow missionary, Elisabeth Howard in a simple ceremony and in 1955 Elisabeth gave birth to a baby girl.

At the start of 1956, Elliot, 4 fellow missionaries and their pilot made initial contact with the feared Auca Indians in the jungle. They used a loudspeaker and exchanged gifts by dangling a bucket on a rope from their aeroplane.

Encouraged by these friendly encounters, they decided to visit the people on foot and spent a few days with them. However, a local man named Naenkiwi lied to the tribesmen about the missionaries' intentions and Elliot and his companions were killed by a group of Huaorani warriors. Amazingly, less than 2 years later, Elisabeth moved to that area and many Aura Indians became Christians!

Jim Elliot

```
F N A H X L G E J S P M H R M
I B J V Y U M D T Q W H D F G
M D R I G T K P M E W G W L I
Y L K Q I T N B J P M E E N N
E C U A D O R I N D I A N S A
D E C N E I D E B O H J A L E
O C M X H W M I J O F E L I N
W A K G J O U R N A L S P F K
N N F E H T O E K F F U R E I
S U C R B G S H I I Y S I P W
T J E A C T E U Y X L V A N I
R K T V Y U I G Z J M L W L Y
E T M I S S I O N A R I E S K
A A K W C G K T O I L L E D B
M V O E W B J F L E M I N G R
```

JIM	ELLIOT	OBEDIENCE	HONESTY	ECUADOR
INDIANS	AIRPLANE	NAENKIWI	MISSIONARIES	DOWNSTREAM
KILLED	FLEMING	JESUS	JOURNAL	LIFE

GOD, I PRAY THEE, LIGHT THESE IDLE STICKS OF MY LIFE AND MAY I *burn* FOR THEE. CONSUME MY LIFE, MY GOD, FOR IT IS THINE. I SEEK NOT A LONG LIFE, BUT A FULL ONE, LIKE YOU, LORD JESUS."

:: JIM ELLIOT, 1948

WHEREVER YOU ARE, BE ALL THERE.

— JIM ELLIOT

He is no fool who gives what **he cannot keep** to gain that which **he cannot lose.**

~ JIM ELLIOT, 1927-1956
martyred missionary to the Waodani of Ecuador

74

"Wherever you are, be all there; live to the hilt every situation you believe to be the will of God"
– Jim Elliot

"THE WILL OF GOD IS ALWAYS A BIGGER THING THAN WE BARGAIN FOR, BUT WE MUST BELIEVE THAT WHATEVER IT INVOLVES, IT IS GOOD, ACCEPTABLE AND PERFECT.'

-JIM ELLIOT

I seek not a long life, but a full one, like you Lord Jesus.

Jim Elliot

Jim Elliot

John Bunyan

30 November 1628 – 31 August 1688 (59 years)

John Bunyan was an English writer and Baptist preacher who wrote *The Pilgrim's Progress* – which many reckon is the second-most printed book of all-time behind the Bible. He also wrote over 50 other books, many of which were expansions of his sermons.

In 1660, the religious tolerance, which had given Bunyan and other nonconformists the freedom to preach was curtailed with the restoration of the monarchy. Bunyan was subsequently arrested but could easily have been released if he had promised not to preach again. However, he told local magistrates he would rather remain in prison until moss grew on his eyelids than fail to do what God had commanded him to do. As a result his period of imprisonment was extended to 12 years, which brought great hardship on himself and his family. In prison, all Bunyan had was a copy of the Bible, John Foxe's *Book of Martyrs* and the company of other preachers who had also been imprisoned. It was in Bedford prison that he wrote *Grace Abounding* and started working on *The Pilgrim's Progress*.

In 1672, King Charles issued a declaration which suspended persecution against nonconformists and Bunyan was released from prison. Immediately he began travelling all over Bedfordshire and nearby counties on horseback to preach the gospel. People held him in high esteem and he became known affectionately as 'Bishop Bunyan'.

The images that Bunyan used in *The Pilgrim's Progress* are reflections of images from his own world. The 'Strait Gate' is a version of the wicket gate at Elstow Abbey Church. The 'Slough of Despond' is a reflection of Squitch Fen, a wet and mossy area near his cottage in Harrowden. The 'Delectable Mountains' are the hills surrounding Bedfordshire. Even the characters are reflections of real people Bunyan knew personally!

John Bunyan

Across

3. Marsh and bog land
8. Growth and development
10. A bad gate in Pilgrims progress
11. Bunyan wrote a book here
12. Wrote the Pilgrim's progress
13. To travel on a horse
14. A County in East England
15. Religious people who travel

Down

1. Tasty and delicious
2. Author
4. A deep bog in the pilgrim's progress
5. High hills
6. Teacher of the gospel
7. Something to read
9. Bunyan's first name
16. An outdoor entrance

> # ONE LEAK WILL SINK A SHIP: AND ONE SIN WILL DESTROY A SINNER.

An idle man's brain is the devil's workshop.

John Bunyan

He who runs from God in the morning will scarcely find Him the rest of the day.

~ John Bunyan

"God is the only desirable good; nothing without Him is worthy of our hearts. . . . The life, the glory, the blessedness, the soul-satisfying goodness that is in God are beyond all expression."

John Bunyan

Pray often, for prayer is a shield to the soul, a sacrifice to God, and a scourge for Satan --John Bunyan

John Calvin

10 July 1509 – 27 May 1564 (54 years)

John Calvin was an influential French theologian and pastor during the Protestant Reformation. He was a principal figure in the development of a system of Christian theology, which later became known as Calvinism – which majors on the absolute sovereignty of God in salvation.

As a young boy, Calvin was particularly intelligent. At the ripe age of 12, his bishop employed him as a clerk! However, it was not until the age of 24 that Calvin accepted Christ as his Saviour. He described this experience as a sudden change of mind brought about by God and as a result, he distanced himself from the Roman Catholic Church. After religious tensions erupted with widespread violence against Protestant Christians in France, Calvin fled to safety in Switzerland. It was there, in 1536, he published *Institutes of the Christian Religion* – a defence of his faith and a statement on the doctrinal position of the Reformers. It was also an instruction book for anyone interested in learning more about the reformed Christian faith.

Calvin was also deeply committed to reforming his homeland, France. The Protestant movement there had been energetic but lacked strategy and national coordination. With financial support from the church in Geneva, Calvin focused his attention towards uplifting the French Protestant cause. Between 1555 and 1562 he sent over 100 ministers to France.

During his lifetime Calvin wrote commentaries on most books of the Bible, in addition to other books on theology and church government. When preaching, he often spoke for over an hour even though he rarely used notes! In his latter years, Calvin's authority was practically uncontested and he used his international reputation as a Reformer to promote the faith in Geneva and throughout Europe.

To the present day, various Congregational, Reformed and Presbyterian churches still look to Calvin as the chief expositor of their beliefs and his impact has been felt throughout the world.

John Calvin

```
F C M L D I X E Y T A E V N J
N Z Z D Y Y H G T Q F Q Y Q M
O K H C A P E S N V E R T S R
I K P V P N R U A M T J N F F
T N A N E H E O T E U Z G Q S
A H H V Q C F I S T L V I T C
V H A O Q N O G E S O Z E D E
L H D W J E R I T Y S B R L P
A L E T O R M L O S B U E V O
S E M P O F A E R C A D V U R
G T R Q J D T R P B A M O I U
C W O T E I I X A I W L S G E
H P F P Z J O Q V B Z J V H H
I R E M H D N R Y L A A W I E
J G R B J N Z A D E J U O L N
```

JOHN	CALVIN	FRENCH	REFORMED	REFORMATION
SOVEREIGNTY	GOD	SALVATION	RELIGIOUS	PROTESTANT
BIBLE	ABSOLUTE	SYSTEM	GENEVA	EUROPE

WHILE ALL MEN SEEK AFTER HAPPINESS, SCARCELY ONE IN A HUNDRED LOOKS FOR IT FROM GOD.

JOHN CALVIN

REPENTANCE IS NOT MERELY THE START OF THE CHRISTIAN LIFE IT IS THE CHRISTIAN LIFE

JOHN CALVIN

"A dog barks when his master is attacked. I would be a coward if I saw that God's truth is attacked and yet would remain silent."

John Calvin

WITHOUT THE GOSPEL
EVERYTHING IS USELESS AND VAIN.

JOHN CALVIN

There is no other method of living piously and justly, than that of depending upon God.

JOHN CALVIN

Prayer is the chief exercise of faith.

John Calvin

John Knox

circa 1513 – 24 November 1572 (59 years)

John Knox was a Scottish minister, theologian and writer who was a leader of the Reformation in Scotland. In 1546, a group of Protestants who had captured St Andrews Castle invited Knox to become their minister. In the summer of 1547 French warships attacked the castle and Knox was taken prisoner. He was forced to row one of the ships with other slaves, but after 19 months he was set free and exiled to England. There he was licensed to work in the Church of England and rose through the ranks to serve King Edward VI as a royal chaplain.

However, when Queen Mary came to the throne in 1553 and re-established Roman Catholicism, Knox was forced to resign his position as royal chaplain and leave the country. He moved to Geneva, where he met John Calvin, from whom he gained experience and knowledge of Reformed theology and Presbyterian government. He led a busy life in Geneva preaching 3 sermons a week, each lasting well over 2 hours.

Knox helped to write the new *Confession of Faith* and the *Ecclesiastical Order* for the newly created Reformed Church, the Kirk. As the religious leader of Protestantism, Knox admonished Queen Mary in several interviews for supporting non-biblical Roman Catholic practices.

In one sermon he expounded the seventh chapter of the Book of Daniel and compared the Pope to the Antichrist. He recognised the Bible as his sole authority and emphasised the doctrine of justification by faith alone. A few days later, a debate was staged that allowed him to lay down additional theses including the rejection of the mass, purgatory and prayers for the dead.

Knox is recognised by many as the founder of the Presbyterian denomination, whose members number millions worldwide today.

John Knox

```
Y J C O N F E S S I O N G S N P P F
T E G D E L W O N K D X U P D H Y A
R N A I R E T Y B S E R P H S G P V
U F B R R E F O R M E D C I O I R E
F A S E R M O N S N K R T L N P E N
K I G I X U I N R T U T O J S R A E
N T J A O U F N T H O E X R N W C G
A H B J N I J H C C H J L Z E M H F
R G S Z K Z R O S T F F O U N D E R
F N L W W S W J I T W S C I V G D D
```

JOHN	KNOX	SCOTTISH	PRESBYTERIAN	CHURCH
REFORMED	THEOLOGY	PREACHED	SERMONS	GENEVA
FRANKFURT	CONFESSION	FAITH	FOUNDER	KNOWLEDGE

UNITED KINGDOM

"A man with God is always in the majority."
~ John Knox

""Prayer is an earnest and familiar talking with God."
John Knox

Give me Scotland else I die!
John Knox
1505-1572

The Scriptures of God are my only foundation and substance in all matters of weight and importance.

John Livingstone Nevius
4 March 1829 – 19 October 1893 (64 years)

John Livingstone Nevius was a pioneering American Protestant missionary in China for 40 years. After getting married in 1853, John and his new wife set off on an arduous 6-month sea voyage to Ningpo, in the Che-Kiang province of China. As soon as they arrived, they immersed themselves in language study.

Before long they were writing literature and travelling around the region preaching and setting up schools and missions. In 1861, the couple moved to the Shantung province, where most of their missionary work took place. They spent some time in Tung Chow and dispensed medicine to the locals during the 1862 cholera epidemic. John also trained missionaries while his wife set up a boarding school for girls.

In 1873, John embarked on a taxing 600-mile missionary tour by foot, finding food and taking rest wherever he could on the way.

John maintained this kind of missionary work, travelling thousands of miles across arduous terrain, to preach the gospel in rural areas until 1887. In 1890, he travelled to Korea and although he only stayed for 2 weeks, his model for a local church was adopted there.

His model stated that missions should only develop programs and institutions that the national church desired and could support, such as:-

1. The national churches should call out and support their own pastors.

2. Churches should be built in the native style with money and materials given by the church members.

3. Intensive biblical and doctrinal instruction should be provided for church leaders every year.

He wrote several books on Chinese religions, customs and social life as well as telling of his own missionary work.

John Nevius

```
F S E H C R U H C Y P W I R
W Y O V E N Y R U W K H S A
I P I O N E E R I N G C N W
P R O G R A M S H M Q R I S
D E G A U G N A L I R E D G
K A M M V I H H E S Q L O M
J J T X B V H N P S W I A L
N O U G F I I O A I C G C X
A Y H G A C X K S O H I U E
L U T N I I O U T N I O S F
P W L D T R I W O A N N T I
J F E W E V I W R R A S O W
U M F A E N I K S Y Q L M G
I G W N P P I M Q F U L S A
```

JOHN	NEVIUS	PIONEERING	MISSIONARY	CHINA
RELIGIONS	CUSTOMS	WIFE	LANGUAGE	MEDICINE
PLAN	KOREA	PROGRAMS	CHURCHES	PASTORS

missions

our backyard and beyond

John Newton

24 July 1725 – 21 December 1807 (82 years)

John Newton started his career at sea at a young age, having first sailed with his father at the age of 11. By the time his father retired in 1742, John had made 6 voyages overseas. He then progressed to work on ships in the slave trade for several years.

However, one night on a ship he was sailing in was passing the coast of Donegal in Ireland, it encountered a severe storm and almost sank. Newton awoke in the middle of the night and, as the ship filled with water, he cried out to God. The ship drifted to safety but Newton marked this experience as the beginning of his conversion to evangelical Christianity. He began to read the Bible and other Christian literature and after some time became a born-again Christian. A few years after getting converted, he gave up sailing and became a prominent voice for the abolition of slavery.

In 1755, he got a job working in customs at the Port of Liverpool and in his spare time he studied Greek and Hebrew, as he felt compelled to preach the gospel. He was given some opportunities to speak as an evangelical lay-minister and in 1757, he applied to be ordained as a minister in the Church of England. However, he had to wait a further 7 years before he was accepted and given a pulpit in Northampton.

In his parish, Newton was revered by his congregation as much for his pastoral care as for his beliefs. His preaching was so popular, thousands of people flocked to hear him and a balcony had to be constructed in his church to accommodate them all.

He was a strong supporter of evangelicalism in the Church of England and was held in high regard by folks in other denominations, such as the Methodists and Baptists. Young churchmen and people struggling with faith regularly sought his advice and guidance.

Newton also greatly influenced English hymnology and wrote famous hymns such as *Amazing Grace* and *Glorious Things of Thee are Spoken.*

John Newton

```
S K X P T G S G U D M U E F L
P E P Z M V U E M P O B Z Y N
K S P J B X Y C A Z Y T S X O
K P Y Z D L T A N J P E P O I
N V I B Y A I R S O I O O E S
E N L B B C N G K H V J K K R
W B A E Z I A L Z N H H E Z E
T G R R N L I Q X V P Z N U V
O N O A M E T G O V N H I J N
N I T C Y G S U O I R O L G O
X Z S M H N I F S N M Y H B C
Y A A F X A R J C C S T S A M
Y M P X A V H H J X Y Y G I F
K A J S M E C B I B L E Z J X
G E D G Y G O L O N M Y H X E
```

JOHN	NEWTON	HYMN	AMAZING	GRACE
GLORIOUS	SPOKEN	CONVERSION	PASTORAL	CARE
EVANGELICAL	CHRISTIANITY	BIBLE	HYMNOLOGY	HYMNS

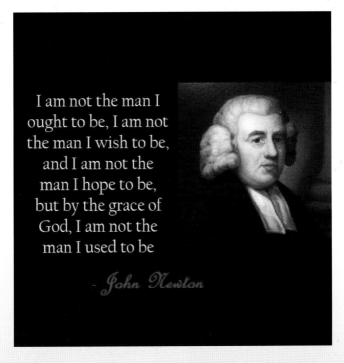

I am not the man I ought to be, I am not the man I wish to be, and I am not the man I hope to be, but by the grace of God, I am not the man I used to be

- John Newton

Although my memory's fading, I remember two things very clearly: I am a great sinner and **Christ is a great Saviour.**

John Newton

When I was young, I was sure of many things; there are only two things of which I am sure now; one is, that I am a miserable sinner; and the other, that Jesus Christ is an all sufficient Saviour. He is well taught who gets these two lessons.

(John Newton)

Weak is the effort of my heart, And cold my warmest thought, But when I see Thee as Thou art, I'll praise Thee as I ought.

John Newton

MY GRAND POINT IN PREACHING IS TO BREAK THE HARD HEART, AND TO HEAL THE BROKEN ONE.

—JOHN NEWTON

John Paton

24 May 1824 – 28 January 1907 (82 years)

John Paton was born in Scotland and became a missionary in the New Hebrides Islands (now called Vanuatu) of the South Pacific. He was a man of robust character and personality and sought to bring education and Christianity to the natives there. Paton was also an author and therefore able to tell his story in print. He is looked upon by many as a role-model for missionary work.

In those days, the natives of the island of Tanna were cannibals. John and his wife Mary were surrounded by painted savages who were enveloped in the superstitions and cruelties of heathenism at its worst. Sadly Mary died from tropical fever and shortly after, he also lost his new-born son, Peter.

Paton steadfastly continued his missionary work despite constant animosity from the natives and many attempts on his life. During one attack, a ship arrived just in time to rescue him and the other missionaries and move them to another part of the island.

John quickly learned the local language and was able to put it into writing so he could translate and print the Bible. He remarried and his second wife, Maggie, served the people practically by dispensing medicines and teaching the women how to sew clothes, plait hats, sing and read. Every Lord's Day they held worship services and many of the locals came along to learn more about the Bible.

Despite enduring many years of deprivation and facing constant danger from the cannibals, they continued steadfastly in their work and sent native teachers to all the surrounding villages to preach the gospel. After many years of patient ministry, the entire island of Aniwa professed Christianity.

In 1899, Paton saw his Aniwa New Testament printed and missionaries establishing a work on 25 of the 30 islands of the New Hebrides.

John Paton

Across

3. To be prepared and taught
5. Two people who get married
7. A huge ocean
8. Little towns
12. Interpreted
13. A preacher in another country
14. The missionary to Vanuatu
16. A common name for a boy

Down

1. People who eat people
2. Motivation
4. The Word of God
6. A group of isles
9. The good news of Christ
10. To teach the gospel
11. An island known as The New Hebrides
15. Popular island in Vanuatu

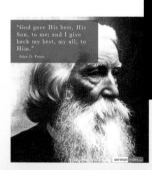

"God gave His best, His Son, to me; and I give back my best, my all, to Him."
John G. Paton

If I die here in Glasgow, I shall be eaten by worms; If I can but live and die serving the Lord Jesus, it will make no difference to me whether I am eaten by cannibals or by worms; for in the Great Day my resurrection body will arise as fair as yours in the likeness of our risen Redeemer.

"At the moment I put the bread and wine into those dark hands, once stained with the blood of cannibalism, now stretched out to receive and partake the emblems and seals of the Redeemer's love, I had a foretaste of the joy of glory that well nigh broke my heart to pieces. I shall never taste a deeper bliss, till I gaze on the glorified face of Jesus himself."

~ JOHN GIBSON PATON

"This is strength; this is peace; to feel, in entering on every day, that all its duties and trials have been committed to the Lord Jesus Christ."
- John G. Paton

"Thus were the New Hebrides baptized with the blood of Martyrs; and Christ thereby told the whole Christian world that He claimed these Islands as His own. His cross must yet be lifted up, where the blood of His saints has been poured forth in His name."
- John G. Paton

WHEREVER YOU SET WILL BE ON LAND GIVEN YOU.

... and over that side of the island all their sacred men were at work trying to kill me by their (magical) arts. Messengers arrived from every quarter of the island, inquiring anxiously about my health, and wondering if I was not feeling sick.

John Gibson Paton

I had my nearest and most intimate glimpses of the presence of my Lord in those dread moments when musket, club or spear was being levelled at my life.

John Gibson Paton

John Wesley
17 June 1703 – 2 March 1791 (87 years)

John Wesley was an Anglican minister and theologian who, along with his brother Charles, founded Methodism.

Moving across Great Britain and Ireland, he helped form and organise small Christian groups that developed intensive and personal accountability, discipleship and religious instruction. Wisely, he appointed other travelling evangelists to preach and care for these diverse groups of people.

His mother, Susanna, was from a family of 25 children and had 19 children of her own. In his early ministry, Wesley was barred from preaching in many parish churches in London and the Methodists were greatly persecuted. One day George Whitefield invited John to come and see his work in Bristol where he was preaching to thousands of people in the open-air. John was amazed at what he witnessed God doing in the lives of poor, simple people who did not feel welcome in the established churches of that day.

Wesley's ministry continued for 50 years. He preached in churches when invited, but whenever they would not allow him to preach from their pulpits, he held services in fields, halls and cottages.

He travelled widely, most often on horseback, preaching 2 or 3 times each day. Stephen Tomkins wrote that Wesley "rode 250,000 miles and preached more than 40,000 sermons."

Wesley practised a vegetarian diet and warned against the dangers of alcohol abuse. When speaking of George Whitefield, he was the first to put the phrase 'agree to disagree' into print – referring to the opposing views he and his respected friend held on some biblical doctrines.

Because of his charitable nature, he died in poverty and it has been said: "When John Wesley was carried to his grave, he left behind him a good library of books, a well-worn clergyman's gown and the Methodist Church!"

John Wesley

```
V E R E L I G I O U S K V
Y P L I X B R I T A I N Q
E H O R S E B A C K S N H
L P Z E G N I H C A E R P
S K C L M S I D O H T E M
E G H A J C P X P B L M H
W B U N O O R M E X T I C
F B R D H J F N E N S N A
X F C G N C G E F O C I E
C T H E O L O G I A N S R
G D Y L A E L P O E P T P
P U R N R R E H C A E R P
K K D X L H C B S R U Y N
```

JOHN	WESLEY	METHODISM	THEOLOGIAN	MINISTRY
HORSEBACK	ENGLAND	CHURCH	PEOPLE	BRITAIN
IRELAND	RELIGIOUS	PREACH	PREACHER	PREACHING

'Do all the good you can,
By all the means you can,
In all the ways you can,
In all the places you can,
At all the times you can,
To all the people you can,
As long as ever you can...'
– John Wesley

"MY FEAR IS THAT OUR PEOPLE WILL BECOME CONTENT TO LIVE WITHOUT THE FIRE, THE POWER, THE EXCITEMENT, THE SUPERNATURAL ELEMENT THAT MAKES US GREAT."

~JOHN WESLEY~

CATCH ON FIRE
WITH
ENTHUSIASM
AND PEOPLE
WILL COME FOR
MILES TO
WATCH YOU
BURN.

JOHN WESLEY

MISSIONS

REACHING THE NATIONS FOR CHRIST

Money never stays with me. It would burn me if it did. I throw it out of my hands as soon as possible, lest it should find its way into my heart.

— JOHN WESLEY —

Bring me a worm that can comprehend a man, and then I will show you a man that can comprehend *God*

John Wesley

ChristianQuotes.info

"Give me ten men who hate nothing but sin and love nothing but God, and we'll change the world."
John Wesley

I look upon all the world as my parish.

John Wesley

John Wycliffe

circa 1320 –31 December 1384 (64 years)

John Wycliffe was a theologian, Bible translator, reformer and seminary professor at Oxford University.

Wycliffe regarded the scriptures as the authoritative and reliable guide to discovering the truth about God. It was this belief that led him to start translating the Bible from the Latin Vulgate into Middle English – the everyday language of the people. He believed that all Christians should rely on the Bible rather than on the teachings of popes and clergymen.

The church bitterly opposed it and argued: "By this translation, the scriptures have become vulgar and they are more available to laymen, and even women who can read, than they are to learned scholars who have a high intelligence. So the pearl of the gospel is scattered and trodden underfoot by swine." Wycliffe replied, "Englishmen learn Christ's law best in English. Moses heard God's law in his own tongue; so did Christ's apostles."

In 1377, Rome demanded financial support from England, but Wycliffe advised Parliament to refuse their request. He argued that the church was already too wealthy and that Christ called his disciples to poverty, not wealth. Such claims got Wycliffe into trouble and 3 months later, Pope Gregory XI issued five charges against him. Wycliffe subsequently replied, "I am ready to defend my convictions even unto death."

For the remainder of his life, Wycliffe withdrew from public life to focus his time on writing and translating the Bible. His writings in Latin travelled across Europe and greatly influenced the philosophy and teaching of the Czech reformer Jan Hus.

Although he died in 1384, Wycliffe was appropriately nicknamed 'The Morning Star' of the Reformation. His writing caused such a stir that The Council of Constance declared Wycliffe a heretic in 1415 and at the pope's command, his remains were dug up, burned, and scattered into the River Swift, which flows through Lutterworth in Leicestershire.

John Wycliffe

```
Q M W N O I T A C I F I T S U J
Y F Y J M C U V Q K U N N R J B
G G C V K I Z R Z C S A B O O I
R Z L V F N P V E W I I N T H E
E K I F V C F F H G B O F A N R
L Y F H Y E R E O L I O Y L O M
C T F X L V V L E T A R P S A U
E I E A Z Y O B A M U E S N N D
W R A B B E B L I T P E L A E B
O O H E H D S U N B F S G R H E
B H G T P N R E Z O L M Z T X L
A T Y T A U C O R A I I Z E A I
P U E R B I T P F V Q L C O S E
U A T W A W S I I X A R G A N F
A B R E F O R M E R O N I P L U
A D B Z M D L I B J N L A J J R
```

JOHN	WYCLIFFE	THEOLOGIAN	BIBLICAL	TRANSLATOR
REFORMER	PROFESSOR	OXFORD	CLERGY	BIBLE
CENTURY	AUTHORITY	BELIEF	JUSTIFICATION	TRANSLATION

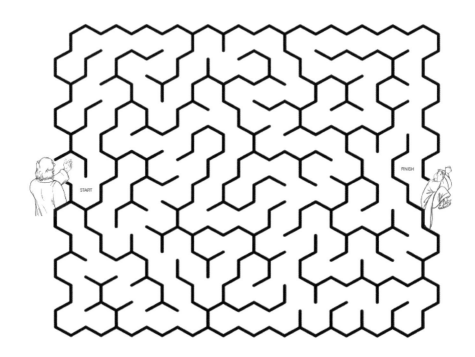

"I BELIEVE THAT IN THE END THE TRUTH WILL CONQUER."

JOHN WYCLIFFE

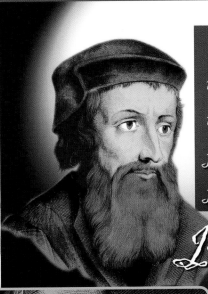

"This Bible is for the government of the people, by the people and for the people."

John Wycliffe
(1330-1384)

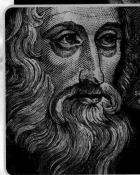

"the truth of the **Gospel** may for a time be cast down in the streets, and be kept under in a measure ... yet extinguished it cannot be, since he who is the Truth has said, that 'heaven and earth shall pass away, but that his Words shall not pass away!'"

John **Wycliffe**
REFORMER 1324-1384

THE MORNING STAR

Jonathan Edwards

5 October 1703 – 22 March 1758 (54 years)

Jonathan Edwards is widely regarded as one of America's most important and original philosophical theologians. Edwards' theological work is broad in scope, but he was rooted in Reformed theology and the Puritan heritage.

He was born into a home where his father was a minister and he grew up with 10 sisters! At the age of 13, he entered Yale College and became fascinated by the discoveries of Isaac Newton and other scientists of his era. He wrote on various topics in natural philosophy including flying spiders, light and optics, but saw the laws of nature as being derived from God.

In 1727, Edwards was ordained as a minister and saw many people saved through his ministry. Then in 1739, Edwards became acquainted with George Whitefield, who was travelling the Thirteen Colonies (British colonies on the east coast of America, which later formed the USA) on a revival tour. The two men didn't share the same beliefs on every detail of doctrine, but they were both passionate about preaching the gospel and seeing lost souls won for the Lord.

When Whitefield preached at Edwards' church in Northampton, Massachusetts, he reminded them of the revival they had experienced just a few years before. This deeply touched Edwards, who wept uncontrollably throughout the service!

The most famous sermon Edwards delivered was one entitled *Sinners in the Hands of an Angry God* during a revival meeting in 1741. However, just 3 years later his preaching became so unpopular with his church members that they voted to remove him from their pulpit!

He also wrote many books including, *The End for Which God Created the World* and *The Life of David Brainerd* – which inspired thousands of missionaries throughout the 19th century.

Jonathan Edwards

```
Q N C F F Z K K W I X S G J A L
E V A N G E L I C A L S O Y S Q
R R T K Q I V Q U N P N X D I C
T J G N O T X W D P A Z E K N U
G S D O A Q H C A T E M J B N L
H R X E D T R E H K R A P A E K
R Q N Q T B R A O O W U U N R E
A H E F W A N O F L R I P G S D
L U C X M I N E P I O J Y R Y W
U O W Q E L R I T M Y G V Y A A
P O M J X O A A C D I D Y M V R
O B I C J O N R D S D G F L M D
P L J H X K N Y C L A F O L O S
N S D N A H U A E P I F C I A U
U D M E F P O P P O S I T I O N
W N H E R I T A G E V G C R O G
```

JONATHAN	EDWARDS	REFORMED	THEOLOGY	PURITAN
HERITAGE	FASCINATED	EVANGELICALS	SINNERS	HANDS
ANGRY	GOD	OPPOSITION	UNPOPULAR	IMPORTANT

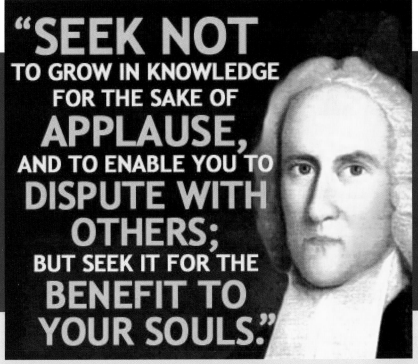

"SEEK NOT TO GROW IN KNOWLEDGE FOR THE SAKE OF APPLAUSE, AND TO ENABLE YOU TO DISPUTE WITH OTHERS; BUT SEEK IT FOR THE BENEFIT TO YOUR SOULS."

YOU CONTRIBUTE
NOTHING
TO YOUR SALVATION BUT
THE SIN
THAT MADE IT
NECESSARY

~ Jonathan Edwards

Resolution One: I will live for God. Resolution Two: If no one else does, I still will.

Jonathan Edwards

"God does not choose men because they are great, but makes them great because He has chosen them." Jonathan Edwards

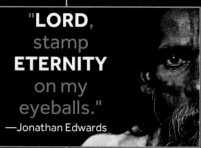

"**LORD**, stamp **ETERNITY** on my eyeballs."
—Jonathan Edwards

Jonathan Goforth
10 February 1859 – 8 October 1936 (77 years)

Jonathan Goforth was a Canadian Presbyterian missionary who became the foremost revivalist in China in the early 20th century. He helped establish revivalism as a major element of Protestant missions to the vast country.

He attended school in Ontario and one day when he heard George Leslie Mackay (a Presbyterian missionary to Taiwan) speak, he sensed a call from God to preach in China.

Goforth was greatly encouraged by his classmates to become an overseas missionary. He was also fascinated after reading Hudson Taylor's book, *China's Spiritual Need and Claims*. In fact, he ordered many copies and posted them to various pastors he knew to promote missionary work in China.

At the age of 29, Goforth and his wife were sent to pioneer the North Henan mission in 1888. Their work was difficult and they lost 5 of their 11 children to disease.

In 1900 during the Boxer Rebellion, the Goforths had to flee many miles across China to safety. Jonathan was attacked and injured with a sword, but they both survived and escaped to the safety of one of the 'Treaty Ports' and returned to Canada.

When they returned to China a year later, Jonathan travelled through Manchuria and it was during this extended visit that the unprecedented 'Manchurian revival' occurred. It was the first such revival to gain nationwide publicity in China and was also recognised internationally. From that moment onward, he left behind his life as a settled missionary to travel and focus primarily on evangelism. He became one of the best-known missionaries in China and was admired by many, yet criticised by some for 'emotionalism'.

"I love those that thunder out the Word. The Christian world is in a dead sleep. Nothing but a loud voice can awake them out of it!"

Jonathan Goforth

```
G R G Y U T D Y R E B E L L I O N B
H O D I F F I C U L T A W P E E L S
S K B N E V G E Q Y T I K W S Y O T
I M Q B W Z I V M G G K A I J U I X
L S T A I W A N R L S S E N K C I S
B C H R I S T I A N A H T A N O J J
A T H U N D E R M S I L A V I V E R
T N A I D A N A C K T H T R O F O G
S P R E S B Y T E R I A N T M S D M
E Y R A N O I S S I M A N I H C H S
```

JONATHAN	GOFORTH	CANADIAN	PRESBYTERIAN	MISSIONARY
CHINA	TAIWAN	ESTABLISH	REVIVALISM	REBELLION
DIFFICULT	SICKNESS	THUNDER	SLEEP	CHRISTIAN

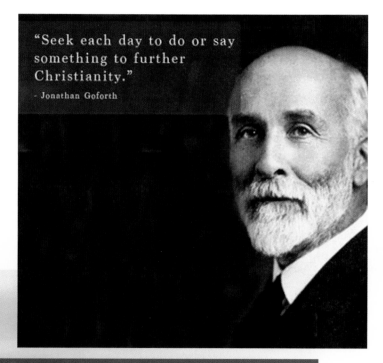

"Seek each day to do or say something to further Christianity."
- Jonathan Goforth

Who am I that I should urge these missionaries to confess their sins in public, when, for all I know, they may be living nearer to God than I am? The Spirit of God does not need me to act as His detective.

If revival is being withheld from us it is because some idol remains still enthroned; because we still insist in placing our reliance in human schemes; because we still refuse to face the unchangeable truth that It is not by might, but by My Spirit.

— *Jonathan Goforth* —

JONATHAN GOFORTH

1859 – 1936

CHINA

So much as one person with a contrary spirit to God is enough to affect all the meetings – that the revival fire did not flow until that person broke and confessed, or the Lord removed him.

Karl Gützlaff

8 July 1803 – 9 August 1851 (48 years)

Karl Friedrich August Gützlaff was a German missionary to the Far East. He was one of the first Protestant missionaries to visit Bangkok in Thailand. After some time he made a brief trip to Singapore where he married an English missionary, Maria Newell. The two of them returned to Bangkok in February 1830 and together they translated the New Testament into Thai. Sadly in their second year of marriage, Maria died in childbirth. Karl left Thailand and began wandering along the coast of China, handing out Chinese language tracts on the way. In 1834, he published *Journal of Three Voyages along the Coast of China*.

When he reached the city of Macau, he remarried – this time to a lady named Mary Wanstall, who ran a school for the blind. In 1840, 3 friends worked tirelessly with him for 7 years to translate the Bible into Chinese.

Alongside his translation work, he founded a school for native missionaries and trained nearly 50 Chinese nationals during the first 4 years. Unfortunately, Gützlaff's ideas outran his administrative ability. He ended up being deceived by a number of own native missionaries who reported back to him false accounts of conversions and New Testaments sold. While some of Gützlaff's native missionaries were genuine converts, others were opium addicts who never travelled to the places they claimed.

The scandal erupted while Gützlaff was in Europe on a deputation tour. Shattered and hurt by the exposure of this fraud, he died in Hong Kong in 1851. Hudson Taylor later called Gützlaff the grandfather of the China Inland Mission.

Gützlaff's writings also influenced Dr David Livingstone. It was through reading his *Appeal to the Churches of Britain and America on Behalf of China* that Livingstone decided to become a medical missionary.

Karl Gutzlaff

Across

2. God's Word

6. Used to print

10. Swayed

11. Something that brings shame and disgrace

13. When something is given

14. Karl's surname

15. A native from Cambodia

16. Small country near Thailand

Down

1. Germans speak this language

3. The Christian name of this missionary

4. Gospel leaflets

5. A nice feed on a Saturday night

7. An Asian country

8. From language to language

9. The capital of Thailand

12. A Doctors profession

All the resources of the Godhead are at our disposal!

— Jonathan Goforth —

Jesus, still lead on,
Till our rest be won!
And although the way be cheerless,
We will follow calm and fearless;
Guide us by Thy hand
To our fatherland!

(Nicolaus Ludwig Zinzendorf)

GO therefore and make disciples of all nations, baptizing them in the name of the Father, and of the Son, and of the Holy Spirit.

Lottie Moon

12 December 1840 – 24 December 1912 (72 years)

Lottie Moon was a missionary to China who spent nearly 40 years living and working there. She was born into a wealthy family in Virginia, USA and had 4 sisters and 2 brothers. She grew up to be just 1.3m tall and was only 13 years old when her father died in a riverboat accident.

She spoke numerous languages including Latin, Greek, French, Italian and Spanish. She was also fluent in reading Hebrew and later became an expert at Chinese.

Lottie's younger sister, Edmonia accepted a call to go to North China as the first single female Baptist missionary in 1872. Lottie followed her a year later and began teaching in a boys' school. While accompanying some of the seasoned missionary wives on 'country visits' to outlying villages, Lottie discovered that she had a gift for evangelism. In Chinese culture at that time, only women missionaries could reach Chinese women, so she was greatly used and won hundreds of souls for Christ.

Moon's letters and articles poignantly described the life of a missionary and urged the Mission Board to send out more workers. She was very concerned that her fellow missionaries were burning out from lack of rest and were heading to early graves. Moon argued that regular furloughs every ten years would extend the lives and effectiveness of seasoned missionaries and the traditional American view of 'go to the mission field, die on the mission field' was wrong.

Throughout her missionary career, Moon faced plague, revolution and war. She generously shared her personal finances and food with anyone in need. In 1912, she weighed just 23kg. Alarmed, fellow-missionaries arranged for her to be sent back home but she died en route at the age of 72, on Christmas Eve.

Lottie Moon

```
L R C H I N A Q X B K U Y C C
N U T V F A M I N E E S E L I
O C M B E G P N N Y T Q B D Z
I C R N J M Y G O Y Z V I Z V
T W O H E E F F O F M G F N R
U Y A N M Q S I M I N D S E T
L T F R V D W A M J P E L D S
O Z A S D E S P E R A T E L J
V N Y O P V R L P S E S M O N
E F D T B A I T A L I A N T H
R I C L I R N O S K A D I T I
J D G I B F E I D K O G Z I K
U B E L V L O V S V Z A U E T
K A N K C E W C I H H Z D E L
Y N I L I V I N G R V Z E R J
```

LOTTIE	MOON	CHINA	LIVING	RIVERBOAT
CONVERTS	DESPERATE	MINDSET	ITALIAN	SPANISH
DISEASE	PLAGUE	FAMINE	REVOLUTION	WAR

SURELY THERE CAN BE NO GREATER JOY THAN THAT OF SAVING SOULS

My sister asked, 'Who is the True God's Son?' The little one replied, in a very sweet voice, 'Jesus!'

— Lottie Moon, 1874

CHRISTIAN HEROES: THEN & NOW

LOTTIE MOON

Giving Her All for China

JANET & GEOFF BENGE

MATTHEW 28:19

I wasn't God's first choice for what I've done in China...I don't know who it was...it must have been a man...a well-educated man. I don't know what happened. Perhaps he died. Perhaps he wasn't willing...and God looked down...and saw Gladys Aylward...and God said, 'Well, she's willing.'

— Gladys Aylward —

How many there are... who imagine that because Jesus paid it all, they need pay nothing, forgetting that the prime object of their salvation was that they should follow in the footsteps of Jesus Christ in bringing back a lost world to God.

Martin Luther

10 November 1483 – 18 February 1546 (62 years)

Martin Luther was a German professor of theology, composer and priest. He was also a monk who became an influential figure in the Protestant Reformation.

Luther rejected several teachings and practices of the Roman Catholic Church. On 31 October 1517, his writings, which later became known as the *Ninety-five Theses*, were nailed to the door of the Castle Church in Wittenberg. One thesis was a protest against the sale of indulgences (pardons for certain types of sin). He venomously objected to a saying attributed to Johann Tetzel that *"As soon as the coin in the coffer rings, the soul from purgatory (into heaven) springs."*

He became convinced that the church was corrupt in its ways and had lost sight of several central truths of Christianity. The most important truth for Luther was the doctrine of justification – salvation by grace alone, through faith alone, in Christ alone. He began to teach that salvation and redemption are gifts of God's grace, attainable only through faith in Jesus Christ.

Luther taught that salvation and eternal life are not earned by good deeds; rather, they are received as the free gift of God's grace through a believer's faith in Jesus Christ as their Redeemer from the penalty of sin. His translation of the Bible into German, the local language, made it possible for common folk to read it.

His bold preaching and biblically-accurate writings shook the church hierarchy and persuaded many common folk to review the foundations of their personal faith. In 1921 Pope Leo X summoned Luther to the Assembly of the Holy Roman Empire at Worms in Germany and demanded that he renounce all of his writings. Luther refused, which resulted in his excommunication by the Pope and condemnation as an outlaw by the Emperor.

He is famous for the following quote: "Here I stand. I can do no other. May God help me!"

Martin Luther

```
Z L I D R O B D E L I A N G
N G Q D M H U E C G Q E X U
O Q T C J L L Z N N O Q A T
I O R O S S E F O R P R N W
T U H L G N L D M R O A V P
A W T A S U E A E T T V Y R
M S G D T T R S H S N P A I
R A K H C T O E E J S O J E
O N E E I P O T N G Q D C S
F R J N M L O W I K E C Q T
E E P O O R M W W F N P S E
R T C G P T H E S E S O O V
O H Y J N N A M R E G H M P
W S E C N E G L U D N I V S
```

MARTIN	LUTHER	GERMAN	PROFESSOR	THEOLOGY
COMPOSER	PRIEST	MONK	PROTESTANT	REFORMATION
POPE	INDULGENCES	REJECTED	THESES	NAILED

THE 5 SOLAS
OF THE REFORMATION

SOLA GRATIA
Grace Alone

SOLA FIDE
Faith Alone

SOLUS CHRISTUS
Christ Alone

SOLI DEO GLORIA
Glory of God Alone

SOLA SCRIPTURA
Scripture Alone

"GOD DOESN'T LOVE US BECAUSE OF **OUR WORTH,** WE ARE OF WORTH BECAUSE GOD **LOVES US.**"

- Martin Luther

I have so much to do that I shall spend the first three hours in prayer.

-Martin Luther

Next to the Word of God, the noble art of music is the greatest treasure in the world.

Martin Luther

"Unless I am convinced by proofs from Scriptures or by plain and clear reasons and arguments, I can and will not retract, for it is neither safe nor wise to do anything against conscience. Here I stand. I can do no other. God help me. Amen!"

Martin Luther
(1483-1547)

"Forgiveness is God's command."

Martin Luther

Next To the Word of God,
Music deserves the highest praise.
The gift of language, combined with the gift of song was given to man that he should proclaim The Word of God in music.

Martin Luther

Mary Slessor

2 December 1848 – 13 January 1915 (66 years)

Mary Slessor was a Scottish missionary to Nigeria who had distinctive red hair and bright blue eyes.

At the age of 11, Mary began working as a 'half-timer' in the mill, which meant that she spent half of her day at a school provided by the mill owners and the other half of it working. By the age of 14, she had become a skilled jute (fibre-thread) worker and laboured from 6a.m. to 6p.m. each day. At the age of 27, Mary heard that David Livingstone, the famous missionary to Africa, had died and she decided she wanted to follow in his footsteps.

In Nigeria, the birth of twins was considered a particularly evil curse. Natives feared that the father of one of the infants was an evil spirit and that the mother had been guilty of a great sin. The natives often abandoned both babies, so Slessor adopted every child she found abandoned and cared for these babies, as if they were her own, at the Mission House.

She also tended to the sick and visited other tribes, spreading the Good News of Jesus Christ on the way. One day, when Mary received the sad news that her mother and sister had died she was overcome with emotion. With a great sense of loneliness in her heart, she wrote: "There is no one to write and tell my stories and nonsense to! Heaven is now nearer to me than Britain, and no one will worry about me if I go up country."

Her diligent work protecting native children and promoting women's rights gained her the unanimous trust and acceptance of locals while she spread Christianity. She spoke the language well and adapted to the local culture and ate native food.

After her death, the Nigerian government gave her a state funeral and flags at government buildings were flown at half-mast.

Mary Slessor

```
Z M C H R I S T I A N I T Y M
T V V S R Z E I Z I X C P S I
F M K F D P H S I T T O C S L
D K Z V V N I I B W E R Q G L
W S R I R C U H N S O M T G D
Z E L H R V Y O S I W R A N J
N G C E P W N R P D L E D I E
I A X N S G O X A M N I W D S
G U B P E S S R T M O E P A U
E G S S Q D O W K T G C I E S
R N M L U Y I R K E R D O R K
I A O F E N F F G Z R R B P F
A L P C S C H W N N V J N S G
W D I P R W I S B O T A Z L J
P J N N I N D U V O C J K W Y
```

MARY	SLESSOR	SCOTTISH	NIGERIA	CHRISTIANITY
MILL	WORKER	TWINS	COMPOUNDS	FRIENDSHIP
CONFIDENCE	SPREADING	WORD	JESUS	LANGUAGE

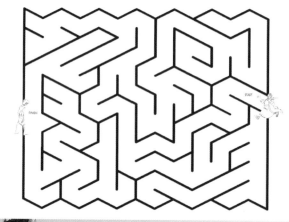

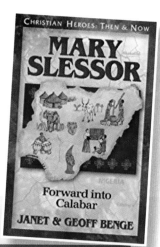

CHRISTIAN HEROES: THEN & NOW

MARY SLESSOR

Forward into Calabar

JANET & GEOFF BENGE

If you are ever inclined to pray for a missionary, do it at once, wherever you are.

Pray on, dear one- the power lies that way.

Mary Slessor

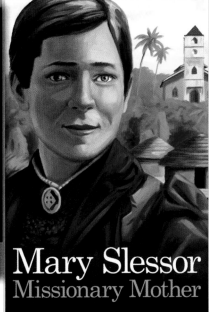

Mary Slessor
Missionary Mother

Christ never was in a hurry. There was no rushing forward, no anticipating, no fretting over what might be. Each day's duties were done as each day brought them, and the rest was left with God.

Mary Slessor

Oswald Chambers

24 July 1874 – 15 November 1917 (43 years)

Oswald Chambers was a Scottish Baptist preacher who was noted for his deep spirituality, even as a teenager. He was gifted in both music and art, but was practical and participated in the evangelisation of poor occupants in local lodging houses.

Chambers considered marriage to be a partnership in the ministry. Biddy, his wife was a talented typist, who could type shorthand at 250 words per minute. She would also transcribe and type his sermons into written form.

Chambers was also installed as a YMCA chaplain. When he told a group of fellow YMCA workers that he had decided to exchange concerts and movies for Bible classes, they predicted an exodus of young men from the organisation. What the sceptics failed to consider was Chambers' unusual gift for speaking and his genuine concern for the men. Soon, his wooden-framed hut was packed with hundreds of men listening attentively to messages such as 'What Is the Good of Prayer?' One day, when an individual confronted him and said, "I can't stand religious people!" Chambers replied, "Neither can I!"

In 1911, Chambers founded a Bible Training College in Clapham Common, Greater London. He accommodated students of every age, education and class. He believed he ought to 'give to everyone who asks.' No one was ever turned away from the door and whatever the person asked for – whether money, a winter overcoat or food, it was given. The year he died, 40 of his students were serving as missionaries around the world.

My Utmost for His Highest (1924), was a daily devotional composed of 365 selections of Chambers' talks. The work has never been out of print and has been translated into 39 languages.

Oswald Chambers

```
D O B U E G A I R R A M E U G
T N A W W M T C C I E H P P R
P Q Y R T S I N I M I O H F E
G N V A H A N M Q S D W I B L
W D W H J E K M G R U K G I I
V U O T M J N X W E T M H D G
D O C O L L E G E G M Z E D I
I S Z Q E M H Y E A O B S Y O
E W Y I E Z H K V N S O T J U
E A M W L D C R Q E T O Q T S
M L F J B A J E U E X I Q R G
N D F F I C F Q L T U C N A P
T F N T B J S R E B M A H C O
E T Y T I L A U T I R I P S O
W P K A G F Y K F W G T E U R
```

OSWALD	CHAMBERS	TEENAGER	SPIRITUALITY	POOR
MUSIC	ART	BIBLE	COLLEGE	UTMOST
HIGHEST	BIDDY	MINISTRY	RELIGIOUS	MARRIAGE

Prayer does not fit us
for the greater work
Prayer is the
GREATER
WORK
-Oswald Chambers

WE HAVE TO PRAY WITH OUR EYES ON GOD, NOT ON THE DIFFICULTIES.

The dearest friend on earth is a mere shadow compared to Jesus Christ.

"Faith never knows where it is being led, but it loves and knows the One who is leading."

— Oswald Chambers

Into All The World

In a conflict of loyalty, obey Jesus at all costs.

Oswald Chambers

Robert Murray McCheyne

21 May 1813 – 25 March 1843 (29 years)

Robert Murray McCheyne was a revered minister in the Church of Scotland, but he died at the early age of 29 during an epidemic of typhus. His brief ministry of just over 7 years made a great impact on Scotland and he accomplished more that will last for eternity than many have in a lifetime.

McCheyne was a man of deep piety and prayer. His desire for the lost to find Christ was so great that his pulpit was often dampened by his tears. He was extremely humble and a story was told that one day in winter, 2 men were working beside a fire in a quarry when a stranger, McCheyne, approached them on horseback. He dismounted from his horse and joined their conversation on the state of their souls. He challenged the men about the possibility of spending eternity in hell by drawing on alarming truths from the blazing fire in the background. The men were surprised and exclaimed: "Ye're nae a common man?" "Oh yes," he replied, "just a common man."

Not long after his death, his friend, Andrew Alexander Bonar edited his biography *The Memoir and Remains of the Rev Robert Murray McCheyne* which was published along with some of his manuscripts. The book was formed into many editions and has made a lasting influence on evangelical Christianity around the world.

McCheyne also designed a system for reading the Bible over the course of a year, which is still widely-used today. The plan entails reading the New Testament and Psalms through twice a year, and the Old Testament through once.

McCheyne's perspective on life is beautifully summed up in a verse of this hymn he penned:

When this passing world is done, When has sunk yon glaring sun, When we stand with Christ in glory, Looking o'er life's finished story, Then, Lord, shall I fully know, Not till then, how much I owe.

Robert Murray McCheyne

```
W P C H U R C H V Y E P S P C S
M S W Q N U D W P J A O C C U Q
U N U K J M I M C T P A O E Q I
R C O O R E A D I N G T K W V
R H P I G B D R L W C R L B R P
A W R R S L N M O Z Y Z A X E V
Y L S M A S Y D X T G Q N Y T C
K W G E U Y E D S N S Z D S S I
F T F Z N J G C R E Y A R P I L
E O U T F Y P N R P Y S P V N E
S N J V N X E R I E U H T W I T
O X E H E L I H S Y T M V U M T
P F B E V O R O C T A N I T K E
I O R F M C N V I C A R I U S R
M W E E T R E B O R M M P V B S
X E M T C D P R J N Y B T H J D
```

ROBERT	MURRAY	MCCHEYNE	MINISTER	SCOTLAND
PRAYER	PASTOR	POET	MEMOIR	READING
LETTERS	PRAY	INTERCESSION	PRAYING	CHURCH

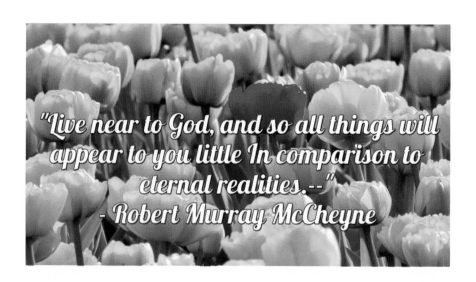

"Live near to God, and so all things will appear to you little In comparison to eternal realities.--"
- Robert Murray McCheyne

I need to be made willing to be forgotten.

Robert Murray McCheyne

"Set not your hearts on the flowers of this world. They shall fade and die. Prize the Rose of Sharon and the Lily of the Valley. He changes not!"
- Robert Murray McCheyne

" Lord, my desire is not to master this Book, but for this Book to master me! Anoint my eyes, that I might prize this Book of love. Unstop my ears, made deaf by sin, that I may hear Thy voice within. Break my hard heart, Jesus my Lord, in the inmost part, and hide Thy Word therein. "

Robert Murray M'Cheyne

"A MAN IS WHAT HE IS ON HIS KNEES BEFORE GOD, AND NOTHING MORE"

Robert Murray McCheyne
1813 - 1843

Robert Moffat

21 December 1795 – 9 August 1883 (87 years)

Robert Moffat was a Scottish missionary who was born into a poor home where he was raised by very pious parents. Remarkably, when he was only 4 years old, he asked a man from his church to lead him in a prayer of salvation.

In his late teens, he moved to England to find work as a gardener. Despite enjoying his work maintaining the gardens in large estates, he had a burden for the souls of people in Africa and offered himself to the London Missionary Society (LMS) for service overseas. In 1816, he was sent out to South Africa and his fiancé, Mary Smith, joined him 3 years later.

In 1820, they left Cape Town and proceeded to Griquatown, before settling in Kuruman amongst the Batswana people. The couple had 10 children and their first child, Mary, would later marry David Livingstone.

In Kuruman, the family lived and worked passionately for the missionary cause, whilst enduring many hardships. On one occasion, Robert went for days without water and his mouth became so dry that he was unable to speak. Often he bound his stomach to help him endure fasting when he could not find food to eat. During this period, Robert made frequent journeys into neighbouring regions, heading as far north as the Matabele country.

He translated the entire Bible and *The Pilgrim's Progress* by John Bunyan into the local language of the local people (Setswana). Besides his early training as a gardener and farmer, he also developed skills in building, carpentry, printing and also worked as a blacksmith.

For the last 12 years of his life, he spoke throughout England, seeking to raise people's interest in mission work. He met Queen Victoria twice at her request and was presented with a Doctor of Divinity degree from Edinburgh University.

Robert Moffat

Across

2. A sleeveless outer garment
5. Mostly spoken in Botswana
7. On holidays abroad
9. Interpreter
12. To make copies and reproduce
13. A big warm continent
14. A boys name

Down

1. Someone who works on a farm
3. A person who fits horses shoes
4. To learn skills over time
6. A country in United Kingdom
8. A person who works in the garden
10. Talent and ability
11. Robert's second name
15. God's Word

"Oh, that I had a thousand lives and a thousand bodies! All of them should be devoted to no other employment but to preach Christ."
- Robert Moffat

We shall have all eternity in which to celebrate our victories, but we have only one swift hour before the sunset in which to win them"
Robert Moffat

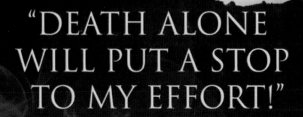

"DEATH ALONE WILL PUT A STOP TO MY EFFORT!"

DAVID LIVINGSTONE
MISSIONARY TO AFRICA

We have all eternity to celebrate our victories, but only one short hour before sunset in which to win them.

Robert Moffat

"In the vast plain to the north I have sometimes seen, in the morning sun, the smoke of a thousand villages where no missionary has ever been" — Robert Moffat, who inspired David Livingstone

Robert Morrison

5 January 1782 – 1 August 1834 (52 years)

Robert Morrison was born in 1782 and by the age of 12, he could recite all 176 verses of Psalm 119. He worked long 12 and 14-hour shifts in his father's shoe-making business, yet never failed to make time for 1 or 2 hours of Bible study and prayer.

He felt a strong desire to become a missionary so he began to learn Latin, Greek, Hebrew, Systematic Theology and shorthand. At work, the Bible or Matthew Henry's Commentary was always open on the bench as he made shoes.

Morrison began to put his Christian beliefs into practice and visited the poor and sick, as he preached in villages around London. He often took time to teach poor children who were neglected by their families and society.

After his mother's death in 1804, he joined the London Missionary Society and was sent to China. Shortly after arriving there he was asked if he expected to have any spiritual impact on the Chinese.

During his first few months living in China he faced many trials and discouragements – He had to live in almost complete seclusion; his Chinese servants cheated him; and the man who taught him Chinese demanded an extortionate amount of money. Another bought him a few Chinese books and robbed him handsomely in the transaction. His utter loneliness oppressed him and the prospect seemed cheerless in the extreme.

One day he wrote to a friend and urged him to join in the work: "I wish I could persuade you to accompany me. Take into account the 350 million souls in China who have not the means of knowing Jesus Christ as Saviour…"

However, he toiled on tirelessly and after 25 years of work, Robert had translated the whole Bible into Chinese and had baptised 10 Chinese believers.

Robert Morrison

```
D C W S X L Y T Y U C G Q Q V
B C S J J F H E X N Z G S Q B
N N Q N R Y L Q O G O D S X Y
O I N E R D L I H C E P B F G
S T A T I A W X X L I K F N V
I A Z R M O H K B R N Y I R T
R L N E P R M I I T N D H B K
R B J B A B B T C O A E A H E
O U H O C A U E I E T U E F C
M E Q R T A S T R N N X K S X
P O O R L E A W H G P Y G R F
R Y Q B N I L X F E G C U L L
S K H I D A H N C Y I J D W Q
L M H E J V F T H I Y W P B E
W C M C S T B E L I E V E R S
```

ROBERT	MORRISON	CHINESE	BELIEVERS	EXPECT
GOD	SPIRITUAL	IMPACT	MEDIATION	READING
BIBLE	LATIN	POOR	CHILDREN	ABROAD

There was a ban on any Chinese teaching their language to foreigners. The Chinese tutors to Robert Morrison, the first Protestant missionary to China, carried poison on their bodies so that if they were discovered, they could end their lives quickly and escape torture.

SACRED
to
THE MEMORY
of
ROBERT MORRISON, D.D.;
The first Protestant Missionary to
CHINA;
Where after a service of twenty-seven years,
cheerfully spent in extending the kingdom of the blessed REDEEMER
during which period he compiled and published
DICTIONARY OF THE CHINESE LANGUAGE
founded the Anglo chinese College at Malacca
and for several years laboured alone on a Chinese version of
THE HOLY SCRIPTURES,
which he was spared to see completed and widely circulated
among those for whom it was destined
he sweetly slept in Jesus.

ROBERT MORRISON

**BORN: JANUARY 5, 1782,
UNITED KINGDOM
DIED: AUGUST 1, 1834,
GUANGZHOU, CHINA**

YOU WILL BE MY
WITNESSES
ACTS 1:8

The first Protestant missionary set foot on Chinese soil on September 7, 1807. His name was Robert Morrison. He was a Scottish Presbyterian, and except for one furlough, he spent the next 27 years in China.

Persevering against the hostility of official opposition and the resistance of foreign merchants, Morrison baptized the first Chinese Protestant Christian, Cai Gao, on July 16, 1814.

Thomas Cranmer

2 July 1489 – 21 March 1556 (66 years)

Thomas Cranmer was a leader of the English Reformation and Archbishop of Canterbury during the reign of Henry VIII. When King Edward VI later came to the throne (at the age of 9), Cranmer was able to promote major reforms. He wrote and compiled the first edition of the *Book of Common Prayer*, a complete liturgy for the English Church.

King Edward became ill just 6 years later and died at the age of 15. Queen Mary, a Roman Catholic, took the throne and accused Cranmer of treason and heresy. On 13 November 1553, along with four others, he was tried, found guilty and imprisoned for over 2 years.

He was put under immense pressure by the Roman Catholic Church authorities to recant his beliefs and to reconcile himself with their teachings. They claimed he agreed to do so and gave him the opportunity to make a public recantation during a service at the University Church. However, he ended his sermon totally unexpectedly, deviating from the prepared script. He renounced the recantations that he had written or signed with his own hand and stated his hand would be punished by being burnt first. He then said, "And as for the Pope, I refute him, with all his false doctrine." He was dragged from the pulpit and taken to the stake where Latimer and Ridley had been burnt 6 months earlier. As the flames drew around him, he fulfilled his promise by placing his right hand into the heart of the fire while saying, "That unworthy hand!" His dying words were, "Lord Jesus, receive my spirit... I see the heavens open and Jesus standing at the right hand of God."

Cranmer's legacy lives on in the Church of England through the *Book of Common Prayer* and the *Thirty-Nine Articles* - an Anglican statement of faith derived from his work.

Thomas Cranmer

```
K O M Q B U R N E D T S H F A
P U K S P B X M Y B R Y H H H
N G B C F P O T G L P D K D Z
O Q H T R S G A Q G W S R M P
S X L H U A W R N Y V A Y L Q
A M V O Y G N E Q E W R L C R
E T Z M V R V M N D A W F V E
R I R A W W C G E M E Z H W Y
T P I S N K L R Q R K K T P A
X L E N O I T A M R O F E R R
S U N E S R Z A R E D A E L P
T P O H C H U R C H H A C Y Y
A P R B T S Q Y M D F Z N A L
K C H B O J V N O M M O C A W
E S T O T V X B H Y R H D L G
```

THOMAS	CRANMER	ENGLISH	LEADER	REFORMATION
MARY	COMMON	PRAYER	THRONE	EDWARD
CHURCH	TREASON	PULPIT	BURNED	STAKE

[Remark as he was being burned at the stake:]
This was the hand that wrote it [his recantation],
therefore it shall suffer first punishment.

(Thomas Cranmer)

"For as the good fruit is not the cause that the tree is good, but the tree must first be good before it can bring fourth good fruit: so the good deeds of man are not the cause that makes men good, but he is first made good, by the spirit and grace of GOD."
Archbishop Thomas Cranmer

There was never anything so well devised by men which in continuance of time hath not been corrupted

Thomas Cranmer

What the heart loves, the will chooses, and the mind justifies.

~ Thomas Cranmer

At the trial of Archbishop Thomas Cranmer :

- Interrogator: *"Now , sir... you denied that the pope's holiness was supreme head of the church of Christ."*

- Thomas Cranmer: "I did so."

- Interrogator: *"Who say you then is supreme head?"*

- Thomas Cranmer: "Christ."

- Interrogator: *"But whom hath Christ left here in earth his vicar and head of his church?"*

- Thomas Cranmer: "Nobody."

From "Theology of the English Reformers" by Philip Edgecumbe Hughes, pp. 241-242.

Ulrich Zwingli

1 Jan 1484 – 11 Oct 1531 (47 years)

Ulrich Zwingli was born to a wealthy farmer in the Swiss Alps. As Luther was writing his *95 Theses* in Germany, Zwingli was doing something similar in Zurich. Though not as detailed as Luther, his article entitled *The Clarity and Certainty of the Word of God* was a powerful tool in promoting the Reformed faith.

Zwingli's time as a pastor was characterised by inner growth. He perfected his Greek and took up the study of Hebrew. His personal library contained over 300 books!

His theological views were gradually revealed through his sermons. He attacked moral corruption and publically named individuals who he believed were hypocrites. Monks were accused of laziness and of living luxurious lifestyles. Crucially, Zwingli proclaimed the cornerstone of all theology should be the Bible and its authority should be placed above other sources.

In August 1519, Zurich was struck by a plague which caused a quarter of the population to die. Anyone who could afford to do so left the city, but Zwingli remained and continued his pastoral duties as he considered himself, first and foremost, a soldier of Christ. In September of that year, he caught the disease and despite falling very ill, he survived and eventually made a full recovery.

As well as being a theologian, Zwingli played a number of musical instruments and regularly amused the children of his congregation by playing his flute. His reputation as a stern reformer was balanced by his excellent sense of humour. He tirelessly promoted caring for the poor, whom he believed should be looked after by the Christian community.

He is often called, after Martin Luther and John Calvin, the 'Third Man of the Reformation'.

Ulrich Zwingli

Across

2. God's book
7. Power
8. A fighter in the army
10. Growing
11. An epidemic
12. Tools to make music
14. A country
15. Friars

Down

1. Songs make this
3. Person in charge
4. Reformers second name
5. Keystone in the corner
6. An illness
9. When people reform
11. A preacher or minister
13. Reformers first name

I beseech Christ for this one thing only, that He will enable me to endure all things courageously, and that He break me as a potter's vessel or make me strong, as it pleases Him.
~Huldrych Zwingli

Unless we repent, are disgusted with ourselves, ashamed of ourselves, Christ does not become saving and valuable to us.

--Ulrich Zwingli

> Christ, having sacrificed himself once, is to eternity a certain and valid sacrifice for the sins of all faithful.
>
> Huldrych Zwingli

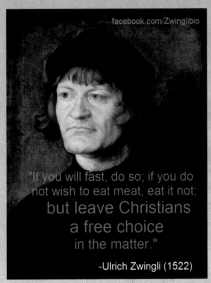

"If you will fast, do so; if you do not wish to eat meat, eat it not; but leave Christians a free choice in the matter."
-Ulrich Zwingli (1522)

BITESIZE BIOGRAPHIES

ULRICH ZWINGLI

WILLIAM BOEKESTEIN

"...do not put yourself at odds with the Word of God. For truly it will persist as surely as the Rhine follows its course. One can perhaps dam it up for awhile, but it is impossible to stop it."
Ulrich Zwingle, Swiss reformer

TheStoryofLiberty.net

ULRICH ZWINGLI
1484–1531

William Booth

10 April 1829 – 20 August 1912 (83 years)

William Booth was born in Nottingham, England to working-class parents, neither of whom were religious. However, when William was 15 he attended a gospel meeting in a Methodist church. There he realised he was a sinner and understood his need of salvation. As he walked home from the meeting at 11 p.m. he called on the Lord to save him.

In 1848, when his apprenticeship in a pawnbroker's shop ended, Booth was unemployed and spent a year seeking work without success. As he was a lay-preacher, he decided to do some open-air preaching on the streets.

Some church leaders heard him and were so impressed by his preaching they asked him to lead a series of meetings that they were holding in a large tent. Booth soon realised that he had found his destiny and became a full-time preacher in the Methodist Church at the age of 23.

He became a prominent Methodist evangelist but struggled to maintain his pastoral duties in his own congregation so he resigned and became a travelling evangelist.

In 1865, William and his wife, Catherine opened 'The Christian Revival Society' in the East End of London. The work grew steadily but was difficult and William frequently stumbled home at night with his clothes torn and bloody bandages swathing his head after a stone had struck him.

In 1878, the organisation was renamed 'The Salvation Army' and was modelled on the military – with its own flag, uniform and various ranks. William became the 'General' and his other ministers were given appropriate ranks as 'Officers'.

During his lifetime, Booth travelled extensively and established the work in 58 countries and colonies. His ultimate aim was to see people saved. The Army's motto was 'Blood & Fire', which had deep theological meaning representing the saving 'Blood of Jesus' and the sanctifying 'Fire of the Holy Spirit'.

William Booth

```
P L O R D A R G A L F R E J W
I S O M T A R M O U R S V G X
G B B B M I L I T A R Y A A H
C S R E T S I N I M M I N R O
D T X S O D P T D E K M G M L
Z S Q Z A A V S R A F A E Y Y
K I F Q T L U P S M N I L F W
W R P V K S V P Y N K L I A Q
Z H K T E W I A D Z M L S T N
I C Y J S R S O T F E I I K E
B Z R B I C P N H I L W N X T
M I B T C K A T R L O W G V L
X N E H C G O D N M X N A E U
C L H M S O E I Z L T H E I U
B O K T B E H F N D P D W R N
```

WILLIAM	BOOTH	SALVATION	ARMY	LORD
JESUS	CHRIST	EVANGELISING	MILITARY	FLAG
MINISTERS	HOLY	SPIRIT	ARMOUR	GOD

"The chief danger that confronts the coming century will be religion without the Holy Ghost, Christianity without Christ, forgiveness without repentance, salvation without regeneration, politics without God, heaven without hell."
— **General William Booth Founder of the Salvation Army**

"Work as if everything depended upon work and pray as if everything depended on prayer."

William Booth
founder of the Salvation Army

Many years ago, the Founder of The Salvation Army, then very old, was preparing to send his annual Christmas message to Salvationists around the world. In those days, communication was by telegraph, and you paid for each word that you sent. Times were tough and the Army was short on money, so William Booth sent a one-word telegram. The word he sent was: OTHERS.

"Work as if everything depended upon work and pray as if everything depended upon prayer."

William Booth

The greatness of a man's power is the measure of his surrender.

William Booth

"No sort of defense is needed for preaching outdoors, but it would take a very strong argument to prove that a man who has never preached beyond the walls of his meeting house has done his duty.
-William Booth

Go straight for souls, and go for the worst.

-William Booth

"We must wake ourselves up! Or somebody else will take our place, and bear our cross, and thereby rob us of our crown."

Your days at the most cannot be very long, so use them to the best of your ability for the glory of God and the benefit of your generation.

William Booth

William Carey

17 August 1761 – 9 June 1834 (72 years)

William Carey was raised in the obscure rural village of Paulerpury in the heart of England. As a teenager, he served his apprenticeship making shoes in a local cobbler's shop. Around that time, he trusted in Jesus as his Saviour and enthusiastically built himself up in his faith by reading his Bible every day. Although he did not receive much in the way of an education, he borrowed a book on Greek grammar and taught himself the original language of the New Testament. He soon realised that he was naturally gifted at learning languages, so he also taught himself Latin, Hebrew, Italian, Dutch and French!

At the age of 24, he became a schoolmaster and a year later was installed as the pastor of a small Baptist church. Whilst fulfilling his duties there, his attention was drawn to world missions. He felt a strong desire to preach overseas, so in 1793 he set off to India, accompanied by his wife and children.

During their first 7 years there, they faced much discouragement – no converts, mounting debt and debilitating disease. However, by the grace of God they continued and in December 1800 William baptised his first convert. Over the course of the next 28 years, he lived out his mission statement: "Expect great things from God; attempt great things for God." Along with his colleagues, he translated the entire Bible into India's major languages: Bengali, Oriya, Marathi, Hindi, Assamese and Sanskrit.

In 1818, Carey founded Serampore College in Calcutta, to train native ministers for the growing church and to provide education in the arts and sciences to anyone, regardless of class or nationality. The King of Denmark granted the college a royal charter in 1827, which made it a degree-granting institution – the first of its kind in Asia.

By the time he died at the age of 73, Carey had spent 41 years in India without a furlough. He is commonly referred to as the 'Father of Modern Missions'.

William Carey

```
T N K R E V I S S E R P M I
Z W M M M V W H Y O S D C R
D V G E O F W I R O U E W E
I R V V N T N M A J O T C K
S E Y S F D K O N P N A O A
T Q E E I D Z M O R E L B M
R E D A R E Y A I I G S B E
I G U V O A O I S N I N L O
B A C Y O B C L S T D A E H
U U A U Q V X L I E N R R S
T G T W T K Z I M D I T W F
E N I Q K A D W P N L L B M
D A O I P O L J B I B L E M
T L N K N O I T A D N U O F
```

WILLIAM	CAREY	INDIA	MISSIONARY	TRANSLATED
BIBLE	LANGUAGE	SHOEMAKER	PRINTED	DISTRIBUTED
INDIGENOUS	COBBLER	IMPRESSIVE	FOUNDATION	EDUCATION

6 He is not here said. Come, see th Lord lay. 7 And go quickly, that he is risen f behold, he 'goetl Galilee; there sha told you.

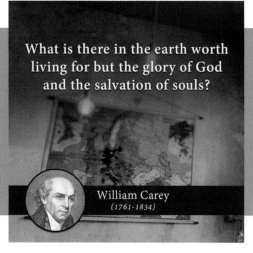

What is there in the earth worth living for but the glory of God and the salvation of souls?

William Carey
(1761-1834)

> I'm not afraid of failure; I'm afraid of succeeding at things that don't matter.
>
> William Carey

MISSIONARIES & WORKERS

"EXPECT GREAT THINGS FROM GOD.
ATTEMPT GREAT THINGS FOR GOD"

WILLIAM CAREY
MISSIONARY TO INDIA

MISSIONARIES

> I was once young and now I am old, but not once have I been witness to God's failure to supply my need when first I had given for the furtherance of His work. He has never failed in His promise, so I cannot fail in my service to Him.

William Carey

William Farel

circa 1489 – 13 September 1565 (76 years)

William Farel was born in France, 5 years after Martin Luther and 20 years before John Calvin. During his studies in Paris, he came under the influence of Jacques Lefèvre d'Étaples. Lefèvre was one of the periphery figures in the Reformation. Despite being convinced himself by the great truth of 'justification by faith alone,' Lefèvre hadn't the courage to join the Protestant cause. He once told young Farel: "My son, God will renew the world, and you will witness it."

From that point on, Farel immersed himself in the scriptures and was sent north-east to Meaux in 1521, where he was given authority to preach. In Meaux, he invited a number of evangelicals to work in his diocese to help implement his program to reform the Roman Catholic Church.

The members of the Meaux Circle had different beliefs on some church practices but they generally emphasised the study of the Bible and a return to the theology of the early church. In 1532, Farel's writings ridiculing the use of statues in Christian worship caused so much controversy, he had to flee to Switzerland for his safety. In Geneva, along with Calvin and Zwingli, he influenced the government to the point that it became the 'Protestant Rome,' where Protestants could take refuge. Together with Calvin, Farel worked to train missionary preachers who spread the Protestant cause to other countries, especially his homeland, France.

It was written of him: "He turned every stump and stone into a pulpit. Every house, street and market-place into a church. He provoked the wrath of monks, priests and bigoted women. He was abused, called 'heretic' and 'devil,' insulted, spat upon and more than once, threatened with death... Wherever he went he stirred up all the forces of the people, and made them take sides for or against the new gospel."

William Farel

```
D G S D W Z M U Q M H C N E R F W X
C D E B S E Z J S R E N X G E S E C
S W I T Z E R L A N D M Y R V V C F
L Z C Y E A H E H O H A K U A R N R
N P F H C R U H C H T I W O N E E A
O A A O G J E J O L U L K B G F U N
F T R V X H W U Z C O L O S E O L C
K S E Q R E F U G E Y I X A L R F E
J T L M Y Y Z V D N F W B R I M N Y
H N G K P R E A C H E R S T S E I Y
K T N E M N R E V O G P F S T D R K
N L G E N E V A U J Q M W O C C L D
```

WILLIAM	FAREL	FRENCH	EVANGELIST	REFORMED
CHURCH	PREACHERS	FRANCE	GENEVA	SWITZERLAND
REFUGE	GOVERNMENT	STRASBOURG	INFLUENCE	YOUTH

"PREACH the Word." HOLY BIBLE

FOR THE GLORY OF GOD

The Reformation

THE REFORMERS

·WYCLIFFE · HUSS · ZWINGLI · ERASMUS · LUTHER·

GUILL · FAREL

"I believe that in the end truth will conquer."

GUILL · FAREL

Is a wise man who doubtless thought he was teaching the truth, but he fell into the hands of the Devil.... Be careful the same thing does not happen to you!

(William Farel)

William Milne

circa April 1785 – 2 June 1822 (37 years)

William Milne was the second missionary sent by the London Missionary Society to China, following in the footsteps of his future colleague, Robert Morrison.

William's father died when he was only 6 years old. He was home-schooled by his mother and later worked as a labourer on a farm to support his family. In his mid-teens, he got an apprenticeship with a carpenter, and while he excelled at carpentry, he had a reputation for cursing and using the crude language he had heard other men use on the farm.

However, at the age of 16, he came to understand his sinfulness and that salvation was by faith alone in Christ. Milne stated that God had used various means to lead him to conversion: the *Westminster Shorter Catechism* he had memorised as a child, prayer, studying scripture and reading other Christian books.

Not long after his conversion, Milne decided to leave the Church of Scotland and instead join 'another body of Christians' which he perceived was more evangelical and had edifying preaching. He was then ordained as a missionary to China and proposed he would "go from house to house, from village to village, from town to town and from country to country, where access may be gained, in order to preach the gospel to all who would not turn away their ear from it."

In China, as well as preaching the gospel to local people, he set up a printing press and opened a school. He also helped Robert Morrison produce his Chinese version of the Bible by translating the books of Deuteronomy through to Job.

Towards the end of his life, Milne claimed: "Learning the Chinese language requires bodies of iron, lungs of brass, heads of oak, hands of spring steel, eyes of eagles, hearts of apostles, memories of angels and lives of Methuselah."

William Milne

```
H M R H O Z F P R E T R O H S C A Z C W
P P T B R O Y R A N O I S S I M Q D A K
J Z F P P U A H X K D R E Y A R P M T X
W C T Y R K L O N D O N W H E P C X E E
V U F K O W I L L I A M E Y C Y B Z C L
S C R I P T U R E T S N I M T S E W H B
L Y T E I C O S I N L H C K D T I D I I
R Y X N D E C N E I R E P X E N R J S B
N Z N P F T H J M D E P R A V I T Y M W
B M O Q D B L O H N O I S R E V N O C O
```

WILLIAM	MILNE	LONDON	MISSIONARY	SOCIETY
WESTMINSTER	SHORTER	CATECHISM	EXPERIENCED	CONVERSION
DEPRAVITY	SIN	SCRIPTURE	PRAYER	BIBLE

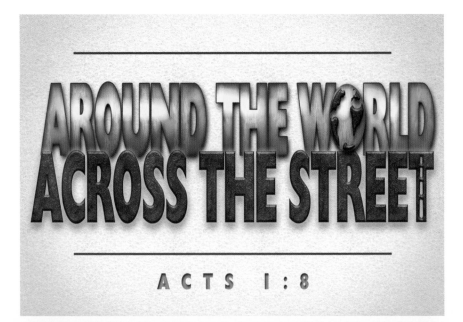

ACTS 1:8

GO

EVERY TONGUE, TRIBE & NATION

THE NEXT GENERATION OF
MISSIONARIES

William Tyndale

circa 1494 – 6 October 1536 (42 years)

William Tyndale is best known for producing the first translation of the Bible in English directly from the Hebrew and Greek texts. He was a gifted linguist and was fluent in French, Greek, Hebrew, German, Italian, Latin and Spanish.

The English translation he published in 1535 was also the first English Bible to take advantage of the recently-invented printing press. However, it was perceived by many as a direct challenge to both the Roman Catholic Church and the laws of England, which elevated the church's position. Tyndale also wrote a book called *The Practice of Prelates*, opposing Henry VIII's annulment of his own marriage – on the grounds that it contravened scripture.

Despite fleeing to mainland Europe, Tyndale was arrested and imprisoned in a castle outside Brussels for over a year. A priest asserted to Tyndale: "We had better be without God's laws than the Pope's." Tyndale responded: "I defy the Pope and all his laws; and if God spares my life, ere many years, I will cause the boy that driveth the plough to know more of the scriptures than thou dost!"

In 1536, he was convicted of heresy and executed by strangulation, after which his body was burned at the stake. His dying prayer was that the King of England's eyes would be opened.

In 1611, the 54 scholars who produced the King James Bible drew significantly from Tyndale's translation. One estimate suggests that the KJV Old Testament is 76% Tyndale's and its New Testament is 83% Tyndale's.

In translating the Bible, Tyndale introduced many new words into the English language – many of which were subsequently used in the King James Bible. Many people reckon that Tyndale is the most unrecognised translator of the most influential book in the world.

William Tyndale

```
K N O I T A M R O F E R
X N Q H H A C H F U T F
P D O P S M A I L L I W
X R S I E I E K Y N F Y
G I I T T L L X I T F H
R Z D N A A B G G N H E
E Q E D T K L I N E G R
E C N P E I E S B E S E
K Y R I R Y N R N M K S
T K U S M E E G V A I Y
J G B L W W S S T G R O
S I B L Q R R S W E X T
```

WILLIAM	TYNDALE	TRANSLATION	BIBLE	ENGLISH
PRINTING	PRESS	REFORMATION	HEBREW	GREEK
HERESY	BURNED	STAKE	KING	EYES

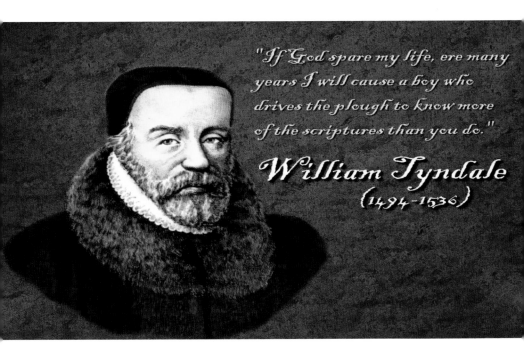

"If God spare my life, ere many years I will cause a boy who drives the plough to know more of the scriptures than you do."

William Tyndale
(1494-1536)

William Tyndale

> I perceived how that it was impossible to establish the lay people in any truth except the Scripture were plainly laid before their eyes in their mother tongue.

William Tyndale

Zinzendorf Ludwig

26 May 1700 – 9 May 1760 (60 years)

Zinzendorf Ludwig was born into one of the most ancient noble families in southern Austria. He later went to study politics and law at the University of Wittenberg but spent the majority of his time on theological and religious pursuits than on his formal studies. He was a noted poet, theologian and ultimately became a preacher.

As a young man, Zinzendorf visited an art museum in Dusseldorf and was captivated by a painting of the thorn-crowned Jesus. He read the artist's inscription beneath the painting: "I did this for thee! What hast thou done for Me?" Zwingli answered, "I have loved Him for a long time, but I have never actually done anything for Him. From now on, I will do whatever He leads me to do."

Then Zinzendorf soon became deeply involved with a group of Protestant refugees from neighbouring Moravia (now the Czech Republic) who claimed to be a remnant of the *Unitas Fratrum* (Unity of Brethren) – a pre-reformation Protestant church with roots in the Hussite movement.

As well as offering the Moravians protection from persecution, Zinzendorf made their village of Herrnhut (near the Polish and Czech borders) a unique religious community. The Moravians established a strong presence throughout Protestant Europe, especially in Germany, Switzerland, the Baltic region, the Netherlands and the British Isles.

One day Zinzendorf met a converted slave from the West Indies called Anthony Ulrich. The man asked him if someone would be willing to travel to his homeland and preach the gospel to black slaves, including his brother and sister. Zinzendorf found 2 men at Herrnhut willing to go – who subsequently became the first Protestant missionaries of the modern era, preceding William Carey by 60 years.

Within 20 years, Zinzendorf had sent missionaries around the globe: to Greenland, Lapland, Georgia, Surinam, Africa's Guinea Coast, South Africa, Amsterdam's Jewish quarter, Algeria, the native North Americans, Sri Lanka and Romania. By the time Zinzendorf died in 1760, the Moravians had sent out at least 226 missionaries.

Zinzendorf Ludwig

```
Z M B I B L E N O U O A K Q C M
R G I Q P P H G L D T A X R S I
K R E S W W Z F X G S E O S Y M
H E M P S Q S B O T I P T W B O
U B N J O I A A W A R O D T Z R
S N Z F P E O W A U H R K H I A
S E P O C E T N K E C U N E N V
I T R S S D S R A S Q E O O Z I
T T O Y G U T E U R K J I L E A
E I T N Y C K D A T Y T H O N N
Z W E A Z A K A P L X C U G D S
N I S M K T Q E M A U W F I O W
Z P T R R I J L I K U D L A R O
K A A E Y O C J A X Z E W N F Z
H O N G X N X A F O Y K W I D U
Z J T H D E N K X H J N H K G O
```

ZINZENDORF	LUDWIG	POET	THEOLOGIAN	LEADER
MORAVIANS	WITTENBERG	PROTESTANT	HUSSITE	EUROPE
GERMANY	MISSIONARY	EDUCATION	CHRIST	BIBLE

SEEDTIME AND HARVEST

The Greatest Harvest of All

'...The harvest is truly plenteous, but the labourers are few. pray ye therefore that the **Lord of the harvest**, that he will send forth labourers into **his harvest**'.

Matthew 9 v 37 - 38

I have but one passion: It is He, it is He alone. The world is the field and the field is the world; and henceforth that country shall be my home where I can be most used in winning souls for Christ.

Count Nicolaus Ludwig von Zinzendorf

For God so loved the world, that He gave His only begotten Son, that whosoever believeth in Him should not perish, but have everlasting life.

John 3v16

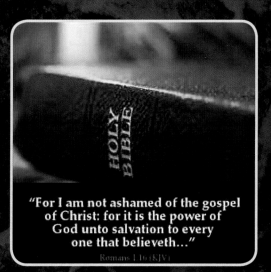

"For I am not ashamed of the gospel of Christ: for it is the power of God unto salvation to every one that believeth..."

Romans 1:16 (KJV)

Jesus, still lead on,
Till our rest be won!
And although the way be cheerless,
We will follow calm and fearless;
Guide us by Thy hand
To our fatherland!

(Nicolaus Ludwig Zinzendorf)

"Lift up your eyes, and look on the fields; for they are white already to harvest." John 4:35

We have come to the end of this little book

and I trust that you have been both challenged and inspired by how God used these 50 Christians to point people to saving faith in Jesus. As a young boy, when I read accounts of what such people accomplished for the Lord, I was captivated but reckoned they must have been supremely gifted or had a privileged upbringing.

However, I hope after reading this book you will realise that most of them were 'nobodies' in the eyes of the world. Despite this, God used them to impact people on every continent and their legacy lives on, even to this present day.

Whenever it comes to the end of your life, what legacy would you like to leave? There is nothing wrong with being remembered for making a good contribution to society, but wouldn't it be much better being remembered for living a life sold out for God? More importantly, wouldn't it be wonderful living each day so close to Christ that when our lives are over we will hear the voice of God saying "Well done good and faithful servant?"

Personally speaking, one of the things that I strive for most in life is to discover God's will and plan for my life every day – then carry it out to the best of my ability. God blesses every one of His children with different abilities, gifts and talents. However, many people are not even aware what gifts God has given them because they don't ask Him to reveal them or take opportunities to serve Him, where they may discover them.

One common trait in all the people mentioned in this book is that they realised they had only one life to live on this earth. They wanted to make it count for God and win the lost for Christ. They had a burden for the souls of people, coupled with a passion for God and zeal to serve Him. I pray that God will light a fire within your soul that will never burn out and your reason for living each day will be for the sole purpose of serving the Lord with all your heart, soul and mind.

A wise man once told me, "When you catch the vision, don't lose the vision!" I pass that same advice on to you.

Colin Tinsley

Other books by Colin

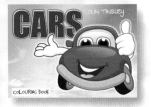

COLIN TINSLEY

PIERWSZE KROKI Z JEZUSEM

WYDAWNICTWO SŁOWO PRAWDY

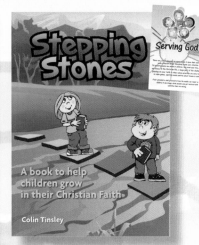

Stepping Stones

A book to help children grow in their Christian Faith

Colin Tinsley

Serving God

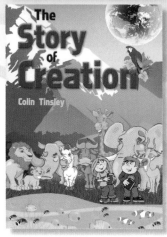

The Story of Creation

Colin Tinsley

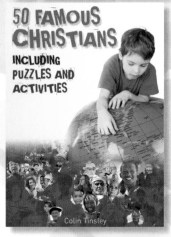

50 FAMOUS CHRISTIANS

INCLUDING PUZZLES AND ACTIVITIES

Colin Tinsley

BOOKS OF THE BIBLE

EACH BOOK EXPLAINED WITH PUZZLES

Old Testament

New Testament

BIBLE

MARTIN LUTHER

THE MONK WHO SHOOK THE WORLD

Colin Tinsley

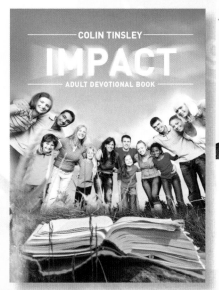

COLIN TINSLEY

IMPACT
ADULT DEVOTIONAL BOOK

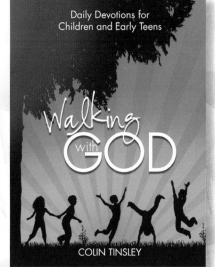

Daily Devotions for
Children and Early Teens

Walking with GOD

COLIN TINSLEY

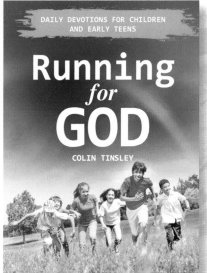

DAILY DEVOTIONS FOR CHILDREN
AND EARLY TEENS

Running for GOD

COLIN TINSLEY

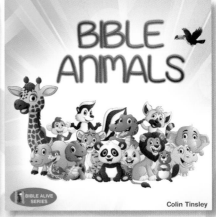

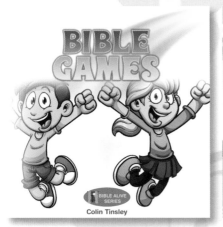

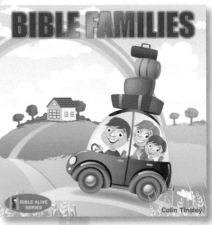

Colin & Joanna Tinsley

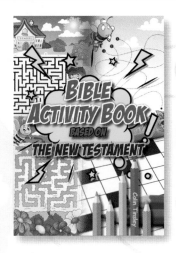

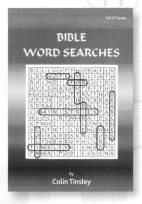

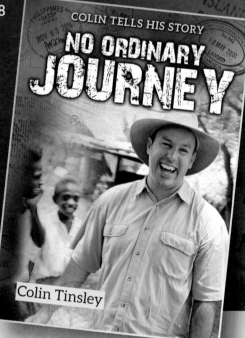